Understanding True, Biblical Prosperity

BLESSED
TO *Be* A
BLESSING

KENNETH COPELAND

KENNETH
COPELAND
PUBLICATIONS

Unless otherwise noted, all scripture is from the *King James Version* of the Bible.

Scripture quotations marked *The Amplified Bible* are from *The Amplified Bible, Old Testament* © 1965, 1987 by the Zondervan Corporation. *The Amplified New Testament* © 1958, 1987 by The Lockman Foundation. Used by permission.

.

Blessed to Be a Blessing—
Understanding True, Biblical Prosperity
Previously published as Managing God's Mutual Funds—Yours and His
Understanding True Prosperity

ISBN 978-1-60463-016-9   30-0067

19 18 17 16 15 14   10 9 8 7 6 5

Kenneth Copeland Publications
Fort Worth, TX 76192-0001

For more information about Kenneth Copeland Ministries, visit kcm.org or call 1-800-600-7395 (U.S. only) or +1-817-852-6000.

Table of Contents

Introduction

In a world that believes the only reason for prosperity is to buy bigger cars and finer houses, a new Church is rising up. These believers are not deceived by greed. They know God's purposes for prosperity.

These believers know God wants to bless His people so they can be a blessing. They know He gives us power to get wealth, so He may establish His covenant (Deuteronomy 8:18) and so we "may have to give to him that needeth" (Ephesians 4:28).

God wants us to minister to a world caught up in the cycle of greed and lack. We can't do that if we are wondering where our next meal is coming from. God knows that. That's why He has provided us "all sufficiency in all things"—so we may have enough to "abound to every good work" (2 Corinthians 9:8).

Our part is to learn how to access His resources and how to use what He provides. You've heard people say about their money and their giving, "It all belongs to God anyway." That sounds good, but it isn't true. Your money isn't all God's, and it's not all yours. All wealth comes from God. And He is the One who has given you the power to get wealth. But He is very specific about what is His, what is yours and what you are to do with what He provides.

The bottom line is this: You are blessed to be a blessing. You oversee both your and His resources. You oversee wealth He has provided for some very specific kingdom purposes.

Silver, gold and all the wealth of the Earth are His. For too long the forces of Satan have controlled those resources, using them to drag men into darkness. Now it's time for the Church to learn what true wealth really is, tap in to the riches that spring from the Word instead of the world, and enjoy living as givers in spreading the gospel throughout the earth.

The most powerful spiritual invasion force the devil has ever had to face since Jesus walked this Earth will be the Church alive to God's purposes for prosperity. They have found more joy in giving than in anything money could buy. They have allowed themselves to become experts in managing the resources God provides.

—Kenneth Copeland

1

A BLESSING OR A CURSE?

Chapter 1

A Blessing or a Curse?

Prosperity. Is it a blessing or is it a curse?

The answer should be obvious. But oddly enough, in the minds of many people, it's not.

The reason is simple. Satan has spent years trying to confuse the issue. And, for the most part, he has been successful.

He has frightened people into believing there's something inherently evil about money. He has promoted poverty by spreading lies. "Poverty is noble," he has said. "Poverty will make you more pious." "Poverty is God's way of teaching you a lesson."

How many have been taken in by his deceptions?

Millions.

In fact, in some way, those lies have affected all of us. That's why it's so important for us to go back to the Word of God and find out what He has to say about the subject. Because until we do, we'll never be completely free to prosper. Never.

So let's get it settled right here, right now. What's the real truth about poverty and prosperity? Which is the blessing? Which is the curse?

You can find the answer to that question in Deuteronomy 28. Beginning with verse 15, let's read what God has to say there:

> But it shall come to pass, if thou wilt not hearken unto the voice of the Lord thy God, to observe to do all his commandments and his statutes which I command thee this day; that all these curses shall come upon thee, and overtake thee: [Now notice here God is about to list curses, not blessings.] Cursed shalt thou be in the city,

and cursed shalt thou be in the field. Cursed shall be
thy basket and thy store. [This verse is dealing specifically with finances. In today's terms, you wouldn't be
too far off if you were to put it this way: Cursed shall be
thy checking account and thy savings account.] Cursed
shall be the fruit of thy body, and the fruit of thy land,
the increase of thy kine, and the flocks of thy sheep....
Thine ox shall be slain before thine eyes, and thou shalt
not eat thereof: thine ass shall be violently taken away
from before thy face [or, thy car shall be repossessed
right in front of thine eyes], and shall not be restored to
thee: thy sheep shall be given unto thine enemies, and
thou shalt have none to rescue them (verses 15-17, 31).

What God has just described here is poverty. And He has
called it a curse.

> Poverty destroys!
> It's obviously the
> work of Satan.

If you'll look over those
verses again, you'll see God
is actually very clear about
that fact. Yet, even so, some
people still cling to their
religious ideas. "Oh yes,
Brother Copeland, poverty
is a curse," they'll say, "but
it can also be a blessing in
disguise because God often uses it to teach His people spiritual
lessons. Don't you agree?"

No, I don't. According to the Word of God, there's just one
purpose for the curse. You can find it in Deuteronomy 28:20.
There, the scripture says,

"[There shall come] upon thee cursing, vexation, and re-
buke, in all that thou settest thine hand unto for to do, until

thou be destroyed, and until thou perish quickly...."

The curse is meant to destroy. Not to teach people a lesson. Not to make them more spiritual. But to destroy them.

Proverbs 10:15 confirms that. There King Solomon (one of the richest men who ever lived) says, "...The destruction of the poor is their poverty."

Poverty destroys! When you look at the pictures of African babies with bloated stomachs and flies buzzing around their eyes, it's easy to see there's nothing noble about that. It's obviously the work of Satan. But what we often fail to realize is this: It's just as much the work of the devil when someone in your own town or in your church goes without groceries or falls behind on his rent.

Regardless of how intense the lack is, the nature of poverty remains the same. It is, and will always be, a curse.

Proverbs 6:9-11 sheds even more light on the devilish nature of poverty. It says:

> How long will you sleep, O sluggard? When will you arise out of your sleep? Yet a little sleep, a little slumber, a little folding of the hands to lie down and sleep; So will your poverty come as a robber or one who travels... and your want as an armed man... (The Amplified Bible).

In that verse, poverty is described as a robber who travels about. There's someone else the Bible describes in much that same way. Do you recall who it is?

Satan himself.

In 1 Peter 5:8, the Holy Spirit through the Apostle Peter warns us to "...be vigilant and cautious at all times, for that enemy of yours, the devil, roams around like a lion roaring [in fierce hunger], seeking someone to seize upon and devour" (The Amplified Bible).

Is it any wonder that Satan has gone to such great lengths to convince God's people poverty is a blessing in disguise? Poverty is *his* creation! If he can con believers into passively accepting it as a "gift" from God, he can steal them blind and they won't do one thing to stop him!

So don't buy into his lies. Get your thinking in line with the Word of God. Poverty is—absolutely and always—a curse.

Now, I want to stop right here and help you get something straight in your mind. I want you to realize that if you're a born-again child of God, you no longer have to live under the curse of poverty—or any other curse for that matter! You simply don't have to put up with it. You have been redeemed!

> If you're a born-again child of God, you no longer have to live under the curse of poverty.

What's more, the blessing of prosperity, as well as all the other blessings we will read about in a moment, apply to you every bit as much as they applied to the children of Israel, to whom God first promised them.

How do I know? Galatians 3 says so!

Christ hath redeemed us from the curse of the law, being made a curse for us: for it is written, Cursed is every one that hangeth on a tree: That the blessing of Abraham might come on the Gentiles [That means you and me!] through Jesus Christ [the Anointed and through His

Anointing]; that we might receive the promise of the Spirit through faith.... Now to Abraham and his seed were the promises made.... [What promises? The promises of prosperity and all the other promises God made to the children of Israel throughout the Old Testament!] And if ye be Christ's [the Anointed One's], [and praise God, you are if you've made Jesus Lord!] then are ye Abraham's seed, and heirs according to the promise (Galatians 3:13-14, 16, 29).

Did you get that? Through Christ (the Anointed One and through His Anointing), you've been freed from the curse. Every one of the blessings God promised to Abraham and his children belong to you! So, let's look back at Deuteronomy and see what some of those blessings are:

And it shall come to pass, if thou shalt hearken diligently unto the voice of the Lord thy God, to observe and to do all his commandments which I command thee this day, that the Lord thy God will set thee on high above all nations of the earth: And all these blessings shall come on thee, and overtake thee.... Blessed shall be the fruit of thy body, and the fruit of thy ground, and the fruit of thy cattle, the increase of thy kine, and the flocks of thy sheep. Blessed shall be thy basket and thy store. Blessed shalt thou be when thou comest in, and blessed shalt thou be when thou goest out. The Lord shall cause thine enemies that rise up against thee to be smitten before thy face: they shall come out against thee one way, and flee before thee seven ways. The Lord shall command the blessing upon thee in thy storehouses, and in all that thou settest thine hand unto; and he shall bless thee in the land which the Lord thy God giveth thee. The Lord shall establish thee an holy people unto himself, as he hath sworn unto thee, if thou shalt keep the commandments of the Lord thy God, and walk in his ways. And all people of the earth shall see that thou art called by the name of the Lord; [How? Because you are so blessed—so prosperous] and they shall be afraid of thee. And the Lord shall make thee plenteous in goods, in the fruit of thy body, and in the fruit of thy cattle, and in the fruit of thy ground, in the land which the Lord sware unto thy fathers to give thee. The Lord shall open unto thee his good treasure, the heaven to give the rain unto thy land in his season, and to bless all the work of thine hand: and thou shalt lend unto many nations, and thou shalt not borrow. And the Lord shall make thee the head, and not the tail; and thou shalt be above only, and thou shalt not be beneath; if that thou hearken unto the commandments of the Lord thy God, which I command thee this day, to observe and to do them: And thou shalt not go aside from any of the words which I command thee this day, to the right hand, or to the left, to go after other gods to serve them (Deuteronomy 28:1-14).

There's no question about it, even in Elizabethan English anyone can see that is prosperity—and God calls it a blessing.

There are those who claim God doesn't promise us physical prosperity, just spiritual. But they're mistaken. Look at the words God uses in those verses. Fruit of the ground...cattle...sheep... land...storehouses. God is obviously not referring to some kind of over spiritualized, unearthly type of prosperity there. He's talking about the practical kind of prosperity that gets your bills paid, buys your kids' clothes, and helps pay your pastor's salary.

"Well, Brother Copeland, it's true that God will meet our basic physical needs. But we really shouldn't expect much more than that."

If we believe the Bible we should! Those verses we just read don't promise us some kind of pitiful little just-barely-get-by kind of blessings. They say God wants to bless us coming and going. He wants to bless us every time we move! Can you imagine that?

Probably not. Satan has had the Church in a poverty mentality so long that it's tough for us to grasp just how greatly God really does desire to prosper us, even though He's demonstrated that desire again and again.

Take Abraham, for example. God made him an *extremely* wealthy man. Genesis 13:2 says he was rich in cattle, in silver and in gold. Just to give you an idea of his assets, the Bible records he had over 300 servants who were trained warriors. (No telling how many untrained servants he had.)

Then, of course, there was Solomon. The Bible says he surpassed all the kings of the Earth in riches and wisdom. He sat on a throne of ivory, had a gold footstool, and counted among his assets 4,000 stalls for horses and chariots, and 12,000 horsemen. Second Chronicles 9:27 says Solomon brought so much money into Jerusalem that silver became like common stones. *A silver dump!*

God's servant Job possessed 7,000 sheep, 3,000 camels, 500 female donkeys and such a great body of servants that he was called the greatest of all the men of the East. That was *before* Satan put him through the wringer. Afterward God gave him twice what he had before.

The list could go on and on and include others such as Isaac, Jacob, Joseph and King David. Every one of those men had staggering resources. And they all got them from the same Source.

As it says in Deuteronomy 8:18, "Thou shalt remember the Lord thy God: for it is he that giveth thee power [anointing] to get wealth, that he may establish his covenant which he sware unto thy fathers...."

Just the thought of the kind of wealth God gave to those men would scare most believers today right back into the poorhouse.

"I'd be afraid that kind of money would ruin me," they'd say.

Would it?

Let's find out.

2

THE FOOL'S DOZEN

Chapter 2
The Fool's Dozen

To truly understand prosperity, you have to realize that there are two different types of prosperity. There is the kind that springs from the Word and there is the kind people bring from the world.

Psalm 73:12 speaks of the latter type. It says, "Behold, these are the ungodly, who prosper in the world; they increase in riches."

Unfortunately, that's the kind of "prosperity" most of us are familiar with. All our lives we've seen people lie, cheat and steal their way to wealth. So much so, in fact, that many people have the mistaken idea that riches themselves belong to the devil. Money is viewed as contaminated, as part of Satan's domain. So, we've just backed off and let him have it.

How wrong we've been! According to the Bible, the silver and gold of this Earth belong to the Lord (Haggai 2:8), *not* to the devil. And the Lord wants it in the hands of His children.

Proverbs 13:22 says, "...The wealth of the sinner is laid up for the just." The problem is, we've let the sinners have it for so long that we've forgotten who it really belongs to! What's more, as we've seen how many problems that kind of wealth carries with it, we've begun to wonder if we really want it at all.

It's true. Worldly riches walk hand in hand with corruption, with grief, with disease and with death. One look at the lives of the ungodly rich will provide ample proof that the prosperity gained by the ways of the world will destroy you just as surely as poverty will.

The Word verifies it. Read on down a few verses in Psalm 73 and you'll find that those who are wealthy and wicked end up in slippery places. They are cast down into destruction and they are "utterly consumed with terrors" (verse 19).

Someone can accumulate a vast amount of money and experience the wealth of the world, but without God that wealth will help to destroy him.

Why? Look at Proverbs 1:28-32 and you'll find out. There, Solomon describes what will happen to those who take the worldly road to riches.

> Then shall they call upon me [wisdom], but I will not answer; they shall seek me early, but they shall not find me: For that they hated knowledge, and did not choose the fear of the Lord: They would none of my counsel: they despised all my reproof. Therefore shall they eat of the fruit of their own way, and be filled with their own devices. For the turning away of the simple shall slay them, and the prosperity of fools shall destroy them.

Read that last phrase again and let it sink in. "The prosperity of fools shall destroy them."

That principle holds true for believers and unbelievers alike. In fact, a few years ago, there were some believers who found out about God's principles of prosperity. They followed them and believed God and, sure enough, He prospered them. But many of them are in worse financial condition today than they've ever been in before, because they used the increase God gave them as a base with which to borrow more money. They bought their way into debt, and they never did anything about helping the poor or giving into the ministry. They are worse off now than when they heard the Word that prospered them.

Does that mean you too should avoid being prosperous?

No! It means you should avoid being a fool!

The Word of God clearly defines the characteristics of a fool. In fact, the Lord has given me a list of scriptures that cover the subject quite well. Among them are 13 which I call "The Fool's Dozen."

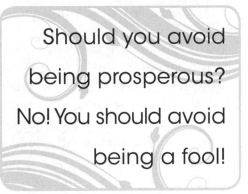

Should you avoid being prosperous? No! You should avoid being a fool!

As you read them, let the Holy Spirit search your heart. If you see ways in which you've been a fool, repent and make a firm decision not to be caught in that trap again. Put foolishness behind you once and for all, and prepare yourself for prosperity.

1. A fool despises wisdom and instruction (Proverbs 1:7).

Let me give you an example of this. Years ago, when the Lord began to show me from the Word about the dangers of borrowing money, I made a commitment to the Lord that I wouldn't borrow another dime.

But when I shared that decision with some other people I knew, they just laughed at me. They could see what the Word of God said just as well as I could, but they were making money by borrowing so they refused to pay attention to it.

Back then interest was low. They were able to borrow money at 4 percent and lend it out at a higher rate. It was profitable for them.

A few years later however, interest rates shot up past 20 percent. Since the rates on the money they'd borrowed were tied to prime, suddenly they were losing money fast. By ignoring the wisdom of the Lord, they literally trapped themselves in a losing situation.

2. A fool is right in his own eyes (Proverbs 12:15).

You can avoid this kind of foolishness by constantly comparing your opinion to the Word of God. When they differ, always go with what the Word says—no matter how right your own opinion may seem to be at the time. If you do that, it will be impossible for the devil to deceive you for long in any area of your life.

3. A fool makes a mockery of sin (Proverbs 14:9).

Here the Lord is referring to the kind of person who thinks, for instance, that it won't hurt him to watch R-rated movies. "That stuff doesn't really bother me all that much," he says.

Another example is the believer who drinks "just a little." "God won't do anything to me for having a few beers," he says. God doesn't have to! The human liver wasn't made to process alcohol and you can't put any through it without ruining it. The person who thinks he can is a fool by God's standards.

Sin in any measure will eventually bring ruin. As Galatians 6:7 says, "Be not deceived; God is not mocked: for whatsoever a man soweth, that shall he also reap." If you sow sin, you will reap destruction. There's just no way around that. "The wages of sin is death..." (Romans 6:23). Not "sometimes is"—"always is!"

4. A fool hides hatred with lying and utters slander (Proverbs 10:18).

Don't go around bad-mouthing everybody from the pastor to the president. That's the mark of a fool. One cannot harbor a critical spirit and prosper in God.

5. A fool does mischief for sport (Proverbs 10:23).

This is the person who tears up something just for fun. I know a lot about this one because when I was a youngster, I was a prime example.

My dad used to tell me, "Now boy, you don't have to squeal those back tires every time you leave a signal light."

I thought, *What does he know?*

I'll tell you what he knew. He knew he was paying for the tires! Prosperity will ruin a fool like that.

6. A fool has a perverted mouth (Proverbs 19:1).

Having a perverted mouth means more than lying and using profanity. It means having a disobedient mouth. It means saying things that are out of line with the Word of God.

Having a perverted mouth also includes the ridiculous habit some people have of reversing the truth. If you took their words literally, you'd be going exactly backward all the time. They see a small dog and they call it a big dog. If there's a big storm they call it a little storm.

Spiritually, that's foolish.

The world of the spirit doesn't operate on what you mean, it operates on what you say. Mark 11:23 tells us that "whosoever shall say unto this mountain, Be thou removed, and be thou cast into the sea; and shall not doubt in his heart, but shall believe that those things which he saith shall come to pass; he shall have whatsoever he saith."

Take note. That verse didn't say you shall have whatsoever you *mean*. No! It's what you say that counts.

Now, I'm not suggesting you should be tied up in knots all the time worrying about what you might say. Just use the wisdom God has given you.

The Word of God says the mouth of a fool is totally full of

foolishness. I know people like that. They're always jesting. You can't get a straight answer out of them.

What they're actually doing is trying to sell themselves socially by saying cute things all the time. But you don't need to do that. You have the Spirit of God, faith and a godly personality to endear you to people. That's all you need.

7. A fool trusts his own understanding (Proverbs 28:26).

The Word of God tells us to lean not to our own understanding, but to trust in the Lord with all of our heart. When we do that, God will direct our paths (Proverbs 3:5-6).

8. A fool utters all of his mind (Proverbs 29:11).

This is the guy who gets upset about something and decides he has to let everybody know about it. "I'll just give them a piece of my mind," he'll say.

Don't do that. Nobody wants a piece of your mind. If you give it to them, you'll only end up alienating people.

Learn to keep quiet.

That especially applies in the area of spiritual revelation. When the Holy Spirit gives you insight into a situation, don't go blab it all over town. If you do, the Lord won't trust you with this kind of supernatural knowledge in the future.

There have been those who have received revelations about someone's weaknesses or needs. They've been given that insight about what was wrong so they could pray for that person. However, instead of keeping that information between themselves and God, they told others about it. That kind of conduct will cause the loss of the anointing of the intercessor.

Don't let that happen to you.

9. A fool walks in darkness (Ecclesiastes 2:14).

The Bible tells us in 1 John 2:9-11 that when we're not walking in love, we're walking in darkness. So, if you have anything against anyone, get that settled. Go before God and forgive the person before that broken relationship makes a fool out of you. It also says if we walk in the light as He is in the light, His blood cleanses us from all sin. As long as unforgiveness remains, darkness remains. As long as darkness remains, sin remains. Only a fool wants that because sin brings death to everything—including blessing and prosperity.

10. A fool does not pay his vows (Ecclesiastes 5:4).

You cannot imagine how many people have made faith promises and pledges to this ministry and then failed to follow through. Don't do that!

If you've already made some vows and some pledges you aren't able to fulfill, go to God and ask His forgiveness. Then, I'd encourage you to go to the person or the ministry that you made that pledge to and get things straightened out with them.

If I were in that situation and I knew that the pledge I'd made was one God wanted me to fulfill, I'd write that ministry and I'd tell them, "I'm not giving up, praise God! I'll keep giving and praying and giving until I've done all that God wants me to do for you." Then, I'd encourage them with my faith.

If it was a foolish pledge, let them know that too. Then go on with a clear conscience. And don't make any more vows without the direction of the Holy Spirit.

11. A fool is swallowed up by his own lips (Ecclesiastes 10:12).

Read what Jesus said in Mark 11:23.

Enough said.

12. A fool says in his heart, "There is no God" (Psalm 14:1).
Most believers would try to excuse themselves from this one really quickly. "Oh Brother Copeland," they'd say, "I've *never* said there's no God." Maybe with their mouth they never have. But they've said it with their actions.

How? By sinning just a little here and there and thinking it won't matter. They'll go to an immoral movie or have a gossip session about the pastor, ignoring God's command to the contrary.

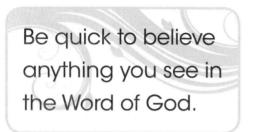

Be quick to believe anything you see in the Word of God.

With their actions they're saying, "There is no God."

Psalm 53:1 connects that kind of thing to corruption. Whether you realize it or not, the more you act that way the more corrupt you will become.

That's an insidious trap and it's easy to fall into, so beware! Satan doesn't care whether you publicly proclaim to be an atheist or whether you deny God by your actions. You'll make a fool of yourself either way.

13. A fool is slow to believe in his heart (Luke 24:25).
Religious people are especially bad about this one. You can show them something—straight out of the Word of God—and they'll just shake their heads because it disagrees with their traditions.

I used to run into that all the time. I'd go into churches and preach for 2 ½ weeks before I could have a good three-day meeting. It took that long to get the people to set aside all the unbelief they'd been wallowing in and have a little faith!

Don't make that mistake.

Be quick to believe anything you see in the Word of God. By clinging to your unbelief you will miss out on healing, prosperity, peace of mind and hundreds of other blessings God has for you. And that's foolishness in anybody's book!

Now you may be wondering, *How do all these characteristics relate to prosperity?*

Anyone who fits the Bible description of a fool will be destroyed—despite his prosperity. In fact, a fool is more likely to misuse his prosperity to bring about his own ruin.

The prosperity of fools *shall* destroy them.

But don't let that scare you into staying poor. Let it inspire you to leave foolishness behind. Then your prosperity can be what God always intended it to be: a blessing, not a curse.

THE GOSPEL TO THE POOR

Chapter 3

The Gospel to the Poor

So it's settled.

Prosperity is a blessing.

But is it a blessing God intends for all of us to have? Is it truly His will for every one of His children to prosper?

A great many people would tell you the answer to that question is "No." They think God has reserved prosperity for a special few. They'll tell you to watch out for anyone who says differently. "You'd better not listen to those prosperity preachers," they'll warn.

Bless their hearts! Not one of them realizes that the greatest prosperity preacher of all was the Lord Jesus, Himself.

If you'll look in Luke 4, you can see that for yourself. There, verses 16-21 say:

> And he [Jesus] came to Nazareth, where he had been brought up: and, as his custom was, he went into the synagogue on the sabbath day, and stood up for to read. And there was delivered unto him the book of the prophet Esaias [or Isaiah]. And when he had opened the book, he found the place where it was written, The Spirit of the Lord is upon me, because he hath anointed me to preach the gospel to the poor; he hath sent me to heal the brokenhearted, to preach deliverance to the captives, and recovering of sight to the blind, to set at liberty them that are bruised, To preach the acceptable year of the Lord. And he closed the book, and he gave it again to the minister, and sat down. And the eyes of all them that were in the synagogue were fastened on him.

And he began to say unto them, This day is this scripture fulfilled in your ears.

It's important for you to understand that, according to
this passage of scripture, Jesus didn't simply make the statement, "This day is this scripture fulfilled in your ears," and
then stop speaking.

No. It says, He "began to say unto them." In other words,
what's given there is a *summary* of the sermon He intended to
preach. They did not let Him finish. What part of it He did get
to deliver must have been a powerful sermon indeed because
verse 22 says that all who heard it "...wondered at the gracious
words which proceeded out of his mouth...."

So, let's look at each point Jesus said He was anointed
to preach:

- To the captives, deliverance
- To the brokenhearted, healing
- To the blind, recovery of sight
- To the poor, the gospel (or the good news that He
  was anointed)

Too often, we just skim over that last point, assuming that
when the Scripture says Jesus preached "the gospel" to the
poor, it means He preached the new birth to them. But that's
not what's really being said there.

In this scripture, we see Jesus addressing different people
in different ways, speaking to specific groups about their specific needs and His Anointing to change their situation with the
power of God (Acts 10:34-38).

He was telling blind people they didn't have to be blind
anymore. He was bringing healing to the brokenhearted. He

was telling captives they could finally be free.

So what good news do you think He was telling the poor?

I believe that He was telling them they didn't have to be poor anymore!

Jesus preached that message to the poor again and again. In fact, it was one of the distinguishing marks of His ministry. Luke 7:20-22 bears that out:

> When the men were come unto him [Jesus], they said, John Baptist hath sent us unto thee, saying, Art thou he that should come? or look we for another? And in that same hour he cured many of their infirmities and plagues, and of evil spirits; and unto many that were blind he gave sight. Then Jesus answering said unto them, Go your way, and tell John what things ye have seen and heard; how that the blind see, the lame walk, the lepers are cleansed, the deaf hear, the dead are raised, *to the poor the gospel is preached.* [I'm here. I'm anointed and you don't have to be poor anymore!]

You may be sitting there thinking, *Well my goodness, I've never heard that before.*

If so, you're not alone! Neither has 98 percent of the rest of the world.

As a matter of fact, I don't believe the gospel has really been preached to the poor in nearly 2,000 years!

We've preached the new birth to the poor. We've preached the Baptism in the Holy Spirit to the poor. Recently, we've even begun to preach healing to the poor. But we haven't preached the good news that poor people specifically need to hear. We haven't told them they don't have to be poor anymore!

Please understand me though. I am not saying the poor

need to hear that God *is able* to prosper them.

Most of them already know that!

Anybody can look around this universe and know that God *is able* to do anything He pleases.

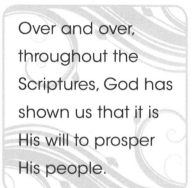

Over and over, throughout the Scriptures, God has shown us that it is His will to prosper His people.

What the poor need to hear is that God *will* prosper them.

That's a whole different message. It takes some faith to believe that one. And there's only one place to get that kind of faith: from the Word of God.

Before any of us will truly be able to believe that God is willing to pull us out of our poverty and into prosperity, we must have scriptural answers to our questions. Before we'll be free to enjoy the blessing of prosperity, we must understand God's will, God's why and God's way.

God's Will

Over and over throughout the Scriptures, God has shown us that it is His will to prosper His people. He demonstrated it in the Garden of Eden when He placed Adam there and surrounded him with every material blessing he could possibly need, including a beautiful wife. He proved it again when He prospered His friend Abraham almost beyond belief.

God's desire to prosper His people is repeatedly evident in His dealings with the nation of Israel. Just read what God said to them in Deuteronomy 8:6-18 as they entered the Promised Land.

Thou shalt keep the commandments of the Lord thy God,

to walk in his ways, and to fear him. For the Lord thy God bringeth thee into a good land, a land of brooks of water, of fountains and depths that spring out of valleys and hills; A land of wheat, and barley, and vines, and fig trees, and pomegranates; a land of oil olive, and honey; A land wherein thou shalt eat bread without scarceness, thou shalt not lack any thing in it; a land whose stones are iron, and out of whose hills thou mayest dig brass. When thou hast eaten and art full, then thou shalt bless the Lord thy God for the good land which he hath given thee. Beware that thou forget not the Lord thy God, in not keeping his commandments, and his judgments, and his statutes, which I command thee this day: Lest when thou hast eaten and art full, and hast built goodly houses, and dwelt therein; And when thy herds and thy flocks multiply, and thy silver and thy gold is multiplied, and all that thou hast is multiplied; Then thine heart be lifted up, and thou forget the Lord thy God.... But thou shalt remember the Lord thy God: for it is he that giveth thee power to get wealth, that he may establish his covenant which he sware unto thy fathers, as it is this day.

Obviously at that time it was God's will to prosper His people in every possible way. Has God changed since then?

No! The Bible says He and His Anointing are the same yesterday, today and forever.

In Psalm 35:27, the Lord gives us further proof that it is His will to prosper His people. He tells us outright that the "Lord... hath pleasure in the prosperity of his servant."

Some people have said, "Being poor can't be all that bad. After all, the book of James says God hath chosen the poor."

Sure He has chosen the poor...but He doesn't plan to leave

them that way. Certainly not!

The truth is, He has chosen the rich too! There's not a thing in the world wrong with a rich person getting born again. The only reason more of them haven't is because preachers have preached what they couldn't believe.

No honest-minded businessperson who's smart enough to get rich is going to believe that a benevolent God will take everything you have away from you, and then make you sick in order to teach you something about Himself—especially when God, Himself, is rich and healthy! No. You have to bend your mind so far out of shape to believe that, it isn't even funny. Only religious, man-made tradition is strong enough to get people to do that!

If you want still more scriptural evidence that God's will for us is prosperity, look at 3 John 2-4. There, the Apostle John says, "Beloved, I wish [or pray] above all things that thou mayest prosper and be in health, even as thy soul prospereth."

It IS God's will for you to prosper!

There were few people on Earth who knew the Lord Jesus as personally as John knew Him. He was the one who leaned on the Lord's breast during that final Passover meal. He was so close to Jesus that when Jesus was on the cross, He asked John to take care of His own mother.

So what he says carries tremendous weight as far as I'm concerned. And he says, "I pray above all things that thou mayest prosper and be in health." He obviously considered prosperity a high priority. What's more, John wrote those words by the inspiration of the Holy Spirit. So they came directly from the heart of God, Himself.

It IS God's will for you to prosper! That's why, as the Apostle Paul said in Ephesians 1:3, God has "...blessed us in Christ [the Anointed One and His Anointing] with every spiritual (Holy Spirit-given) blessing in the heavenly realm!" *(The Amplified Bible).*

Now some people have let the word "spiritual" there in that verse throw them. "God's not talking about material blessings," they say, "just spiritual." But let me tell you something: You can't separate those two. That's why Jesus says, "But seek ye first the kingdom of God, and his righteousness; and all these things shall be added unto you" (Matthew 6:33). He knows the spiritual realm will bring blessing in the material realm.

God is a Spirit and He created the material world. Since the moment God spoke it into existence, that world has been governed by spiritual forces. That's why when the devil corrupted it spiritually, physical corruption broke out as well. Death, disease, poverty and pain were the physical effects of man's spiritual fall.

In other words, the physical world cannot operate independently from the spiritual world. What happens in the one is simply a reflection of what happens in the other.

Look at Psalm 112:1, 3 and you'll see what I mean. "Praise ye the Lord. Blessed is the man that feareth the Lord, that delighteth greatly in his commandments.... Wealth and riches shall be in his house: and his righteousness endureth for ever."

Obviously, your spiritual standing profoundly affects your financial standing. That's why, when you get hold of the gospel and begin to prosper spiritually, you can begin to prosper physically and materially as well. Of course, you don't *have* to. God won't force prosperity on you. But if you're willing to receive it by faith, He'll provide it.

I'll never forget the time Gloria discovered that scripture. We didn't have much money at the time. The walls in our house were as bare as they could be. But she was ready to decorate.

So she took that promise, "Wealth and riches shall be in his house," and laid claim to it by faith. Then she added to it the promise in Proverbs 24:3-4 which says, "Through skillful and godly wisdom is a house [a life, a home, a family] built, and by understanding it is established [on a sound and good foundation]. And by knowledge shall the chambers [of its every area] be filled with all precious and pleasant riches" (*The Amplified Bible*). Our home, over the years, has been thoroughly furnished by that scripture and it's still working in our lives today.

You see, according to the Word of God we not only have hope through Jesus in the kingdom to come, but also we have hope in the here and now. So many believers don't understand that. They continue to make some kind of artificial separation, putting material things on one side and spiritual things on the other.

Tragically, that attitude has cost us countless souls! One of the main reasons we've never won the world to Jesus is that we've never shown them how God could help them deal with the material monster that's eating them alive right now. Instead, we've acted like God was so far above material things that He wouldn't have anything to do with them. The ironic thing is, He created those very material things for His family in the first place!

Certainly God wants to save people from hell and get them into heaven, but He also wants to save them from the hell the devil has created right here on this Earth. In fact, the word *soteria* (translated "salvation" in English) literally means deliverance from temporary evils.

God wants people to have that deliverance—now! That's why He's instructed me to take this message to the poorest people in the world.

There have been some who've tried to discourage me from

obeying that instruction. "You can preach that prosperity stuff in the United States, but don't you preach it over here," they said. "It won't work. Our people are too poor."

But I'm doing it anyway, and it's working in the most poverty-stricken nations in the world, just like God said it would. As a matter of fact, most of the time it works better there than it does in America.

The reason is simple. In many "less civilized" countries, people still realize how closely physical things and spiritual things are related. When someone stands up in front of an African tribesman, for example, and says that through Jesus he has a blood covenant with Almighty God, he knows far more about what that means than the average American ever will. He's been cutting covenants for years with the blood of chickens and goats. So when he finds out God's blood has been shed for him, he is immediately interested and very excited.

An African believer will hear someone say, "You can raise the dead through the power of that blood covenant," and he'll go dig up the cemetery if you don't watch him. There, a guy who hasn't been saved even a week will jump right up and start doing miracles in the Name of Jesus. He realizes just how real the things of the spirit realm are.

You've heard all the stories about the great and marvelous miracles that happen in places like that. Well, what do you think will happen when we go there and preach the gospel to the poor? They'll put a lot of these so-called "rich Americans" to shame!

For example, if a man from a country in Africa goes to a tent meeting and is saved, it's the first time in his life he's had any hope. He gets baptized. Next thing you know someone's showing him how to pray in the Name of Jesus according to the covenant of blood. Glory to God, he's so excited he can hardly stand it.

Then, on top of it all, you tell him God wants to prosper him!

Prosperity doesn't mean a Cadillac to this guy. It means God will show him how to get some water on his scorched village. It

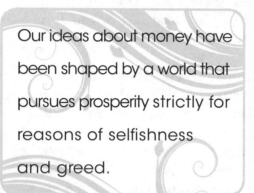

Our ideas about money have been shaped by a world that pursues prosperity strictly for reasons of selfishness and greed.

means God will do something about the alkaline poison that's ruined his land. It means God will show him how to grow crops, so his family can prosper instead of starving to death.

Should you really tell a man like that—a man in one of the poorest countries in the world, a man with no natural hope at all—that God wants to prosper His people? You bet you should!

Then once you peel him off the roof, you should tell him why.

God's Why

What *is* God's reason for prospering His people? Is it so we can be more comfortable? So we can buy bigger cars and finer houses?

Be honest now. It's difficult to even imagine any other reason for prosperity, isn't it? That's because our ideas about money have been shaped by a world that pursues prosperity strictly for reasons of selfishness and greed.

But in the Word of God, the Lord provides us with two entirely different purposes.

Look again at Deuteronomy 8:18, and you'll see the first one. "But thou shalt remember the Lord thy God: for it is he that giveth thee power to get wealth, that he may establish his covenant...."

God intends for us to use the wealth He gives us to help establish His covenant on the Earth. Jesus told us to go into all the world and preach the gospel, and that takes money—whether you're preaching it from the pulpit of a local church, beneath a tent in Africa or on national television.

You'll find God's second purpose for prosperity in Ephesians 4:28. "Let him that stole steal no more: but rather let him labour, working with his hands the thing which is good, that he may have to give to him that needeth."

- Establishing God's covenant on the Earth
- Giving to those in need

That's what prosperity is really all about.

It's absolutely tragic how foreign that is to most people's thinking. I've actually heard people say, "I don't need much prosperity. I'm a simple person with a simple life. So I just ask God for enough to meet my needs."

They think that's humility, but it's not. It's selfishness!

They could ask God for a million dollars, take out just enough to meet their simple needs, and give the rest away. But that doesn't even occur to them because, when it comes to money, they've been brainwashed by a world that says if you have it, you have to keep it!

Without realizing it, they're actually saying, "All I care about is meeting my own needs. I have no ambition to help meet anyone else's."

That philosophy has tragically crippled the ministry of Jesus Christ on the Earth today. It has caused preachers to have to set aside their calling and get secular jobs just to survive. It has handicapped churches and stunted the growth of ministries that could have reached thousands for the Lord.

On top of it all, those same folks who aren't willing to ask God for money to give into the ministry will criticize the first sign of prosperity they see in the life of a preacher. "My heavens," they'll gasp, "that preacher has an airplane!"

It never occurs to them that he can reach more people for Jesus that way. That plane may have multiplied that preacher's capacity for ministry by 70 percent, but they'll never know it. They'll be too busy worrying and fussing over what could happen if the preacher gets too comfortable.

If you're wise, you'll want the ministers of God to be comfortable. One of them may run across your son or your daughter out there somewhere in need of spiritual help. When he does, you'd better hope he's not so tired and sore from riding in the back of a bus that he can't think of anything to say to them.

Take care of the preachers who've blessed you. Take care of your pastor. He's the shepherd and the bishop of your soul. Don't make him work nights just to make ends meet. Pay him well so he'll have plenty of time to spend in prayer and in the Word. Your spiritual well-being is wrapped up in his!

Some people say, "Well, Jesus' ministry was poor and He got along just fine." That's ridiculous. It would have been impossible for Jesus to be poor! All the way through the Old Testament, God promised material blessings to anyone who would walk perfect and upright before Him. If God had failed to bless Jesus financially, He would have been breaking His own Word.

Look what happened when Jesus got involved in Simon Peter's fishing expedition in Luke 5. Peter caught enough fish to sink two boats.

In Luke 8:3, the Word records that many people "...ministered to and provided for Him [Jesus] and them out of their property and personal belongings" (The Amplified Bible). Jesus had so much money coming in and going out through His ministry that He had to appoint a treasurer. That's what Judas was. There was enough money in that treasury for Judas to steal from it without the money being missed.

But Jesus didn't store up all that money for Himself. He gave it to meet the needs of those around Him. He had such a reputation for giving, that on the night of that last Passover, when Judas left so abruptly, the disciples assumed that Jesus had sent him out to give to the poor.

Can you imagine how much and how often Jesus must have given to the poor for the disciples to make that assumption?

Jesus never built a worldly empire for Himself. But that doesn't mean He was poor. It means He was the greatest giver who ever walked the face of this Earth. And it's about time we started following in His footsteps.

It's time we stopped piously pretending that money isn't important. It is. You know it and God knows it. Why do you think He said that where your money is, there will your heart be also? People's hearts are closely related to their pocketbooks.

In fact, if you'll start giving, if you'll start taking care of the needs in other people's pocketbooks, you'll be far more likely to win their hearts. You may not actually be able to use money to buy a fellow into the kingdom of God, but you can certainly get his attention with it.

What do you think will happen to the heart of a starving nation when you bring in a 747 full of medicine and clothes and food in the Name of Jesus? What will happen when you bring in doctors and nurses for them free of charge?

I'll tell you what will happen. The hearts of those people will soften. They will be willing to listen to what you have to say about Jesus. In fact, they'll let you preach about anybody you want to if you will just keep them from starving. Believe me, a plane load of goods will go a long way toward getting a country full of poor people born again.

I have a friend, Reinhard Bonnke, who has a wonderful ministry among the African people. Literally hundreds of thousands have been born again and baptized with the Holy Ghost in his meetings. A few years ago, he sat down and compared the number of people who'd been saved through that ministry with its expenses.

Do you know what he learned? He found at that time it cost his ministry $3 to win a soul for the Lord Jesus Christ on the African continent.

Three dollars a soul! Don't ever let anyone tell you it's wrong for you to want to prosper. It's wrong for you *not* to want to prosper when that prosperity can mean the difference between heaven and hell for millions of people.

How dare we be satisfied to earn just enough to get us by! How dare we ignore God's promises of prosperity when people all around us are physically and spiritually starving to death! Once you think that way, you'll begin to see everything differently, even the Scriptures. Take Philippians 4:19, for example. It says, "My God shall supply all your need according to his riches in glory by Christ Jesus."

Now, considering everything we've just talked about, what are your needs? Rent money? Groceries? A new car?

No!

You need money to help preach the gospel. You need money to help feed the poor. You need money so you can give to those in need.

Does that mean your personal needs will go unmet?

Absolutely not!

Jesus made that clear when He preached the Sermon on the Mount. Just listen to what He said:

No man can serve two masters: for either he will hate the one, and love the other; or else he will hold to the one, and despise the other. Ye cannot serve God and mammon. Therefore I say unto you, Take no thought for your life, what ye shall eat, or what ye shall drink; nor yet for your body, what ye shall put on. Is not the life more than meat, and the body than raiment?

Behold the fowls of the air: for they sow not, neither do they reap, nor gather into barns; yet your heavenly Father feedeth them. Are ye not much better than they?... And why take ye thought for raiment? Consider the lilies of the field, how they grow; they toil not, neither do they spin: And yet I say unto you, That even Solomon in all his glory was not arrayed like one of these.

Wherefore, if God so clothe the grass of the field, which today is, and tomorrow is cast into the oven, shall he not much more clothe you, O ye of little faith? Therefore take no thought, saying, What shall we eat? or, What shall we drink? or, Wherewithal shall we be clothed? (For after all these things do the Gentiles seek:) for your heavenly Father knoweth that ye have need of all these things. But seek ye first the kingdom of God, and his righteousness; and all these things shall be added unto you (Matthew 6:24-33).

Some people have very low expectations of what God will provide for them materially because they miss the full meaning of that scripture. It's not that they don't trust Him to feed and clothe them, it's just that they don't trust Him to feed and clothe them very *well!*

Somehow they have the idea that God is an old miser who will do little more than put rags on their backs and beans on their tables. But that's not what Jesus told us. He said God would clothe us better than He clothed Solomon!

That one statement alone proves that God wants to do more than just meet our basic needs. He loves us abundantly, beyond our ability to comprehend. And He wants to bless us abundantly. I know that from personal experience.

A few years ago I came home and found a new Mercedes automobile parked in my driveway. It had been given to me by a man who'd been blessed by the Lord through my ministry.

Now I didn't *need* that car. I was driving a pickup that suited me just fine.

My first instinct was to sell it and put the money into the ministry. But when I went to the Lord about it, He said, *Don't you do that! You promised the people that you'd use their gifts according to their instructions. He did not give you that car to sell. If someone gives you money for your television ministry, you promised not to use it to pay the rent on your building* (years before we moved to our Eagle Mountain headquarters) *but to put it into television. This car situation is no different.*

It was true. The man who had given me the car had specifically told me that he was giving it to me to drive and enjoy—not to sell.

Still, I was baffled and, quite honestly, a little embarrassed about having such a fine car.

"Lord," I said, "I didn't need it. I hadn't asked You for it. I wasn't even believing for it. What is it doing here?"

Then the Lord spoke up on the inside of me. *Have you ever read the scripture in Deuteronomy 28:2 that says "All these blessings shall come on thee, and overtake thee, if thou shalt hearken unto the*

God loves us abundantly, above our ability to comprehend. And He wants to bless us abundantly.

voice of the Lord thy God"?
"Yes," I answered.

Well, son, He said, *You've just been overtaken! If you'll remember how many vehicles you and Gloria have given since you've been in the ministry, you'll see why.*

So, Gloria and I, along with our daughter Kellie, began to try to remember all that we'd given away. Back then the total included 14 automobiles, four or five trucks, and several airplanes. I'd never really thought about it until then. I'd just given as God had instructed me. He'd always provided the funds, so it didn't seem to me I was doing anything all that great.

But God appreciated it anyway.

"Brother Copeland," you may say, "do you mean to tell me God gave you those expensive cars just for you to enjoy them?"

Yes. That's exactly what I mean.

In fact, in 1 Timothy 6:17, the Lord says point blank that He "giveth us richly all things to enjoy." God is a loving Father. He gets great pleasure from blessing His children. He's abundantly generous where we're concerned. But don't let that worry you. He can afford it. And although we should receive and enjoy those blessings as He gives them to us, we should never let them distract us from the true purpose for prosperity which is to meet the needs of others.

Chances are, you've spent years learning the world's way of dealing with prosperity, so it may take you awhile to turn your attitude around. But don't worry about it. Just get busy giving.

Renew your mind with the Word of God. Then the motivations will take care of themselves.

You may need to set aside a special bank account and commit everything in it to the poor. Start praying about where God wants you to put it and as soon as He shows you a place—put it there!

Once you start doing that, you'll begin to catch on. Before long, you'll discover that there's great joy in giving. You'll give everything you have and then earn some more for the fun of giving it away.

You'll go out and find some poor old fellow who doesn't have a dime. You'll give him some clothes and some food and help him find a place to live. Then, you'll start telling him about Jesus. You'll show him how to get born again and baptized in the Holy Ghost. Then you'll start teaching him the laws of prosperity and showing him how to give to others.

Next thing you know, he'll be prospering. Then he'll go out and find some other poor guy who doesn't have a dime and follow in your footsteps.

When you start getting involved in that kind of thing, you'll have a whole new attitude about going to work in the morning. Instead of working to live you'll start working to give. There's more joy in that than in all the fur coats and fancy cars that money could ever buy.

God's Way

Now, let's get practical.

You know God is *willing* to prosper you. You know *why* He will prosper you. But you're still not exactly sure *how* He will do it.

Will He put a check in the mail? Or start floating twenty dollar bills down from the trees?

No. Remember what 3 John 2 said? "Beloved, I wish above all things that thou mayest prosper and be in health, even as thy soul prospereth."

God will bless you materially by causing your *soul* to prosper. He will plant the seed of prosperity in your mind, in your will and in your emotions. He will give you understanding of the laws of abundance. Then as you put them into action and allow them to grow, you'll eventually reap a great financial harvest.

Go to the book of Genesis and read the story of Joseph. It's a perfect demonstration of what I'm talking about.

When Joseph was sold as a slave to the Egyptians, he didn't have a dime to his name. He didn't even have his freedom! But, right in the middle of his slavery, God gave Joseph such wisdom and ability that he made his slave master rich. As a result, the man put Joseph in charge of all his possessions.

Later the slave master's wife got mad at Joseph and he ended up in prison. There's really not much opportunity for advancement in prison, is there? But again, God prospered Joseph's soul. He gave him insight that no other man in Egypt had. As a result, he ended up on Pharaoh's staff—not as a slave, but as the most honored man in the entire country next to Pharaoh himself.

He rode along in a chariot and people literally bowed down before him. During a worldwide famine, Joseph was in charge of *all* the food. Now that's prosperity!

How did God accomplish that? By prospering Joseph's soul. No matter how dismal Joseph's situation became, no matter how impossible his problems, God was able to reveal the spiritual secrets that would open the door of success for him.

That's what makes God's method of prospering so exciting. It works anywhere and everywhere! It will work in the poorest countries on the face of this Earth just like it will work here in the United States.

I've seen it happen!

Some years ago, for example, in Mozambique there was a pastor who got hold of the gospel to the poor. He found out that God would prosper His people. At that time there were hardly any resources left in Mozambique. People everywhere were starving.

But this one pastor believed that God would prosper His people, and he and his congregation made it through that horrible time by their faith.

Another striking example of God's ability to prosper anyone anywhere took place a few years ago in an African village named Rungai. The village was in terrible shape. There had been a long drought. In fact, the little reservoir that had once supplied the village with water had been empty for so long that the dam there was broken and crumbling.

There didn't seem to be any hope for the people in Rungai until a local pastor got hold of God's Word, and God prospered his soul about supernatural prosperity.

God told him to get the believers in the village together and begin rebuilding their dam. It looked like a ridiculous thing to do. There hadn't been any rain for ages and there wasn't a cloud in the sky. Yet God had given them the secret to success and, in faith and obedience, they acted on it.

Not long after the job was completed, a rain cloud formed right over their little reservoir, filling it with water.

But that's not the end of the story!

You see, the soil at Rungai had been so parched, so full of alkaline and poison, that nothing much would grow in it. But, after that rain, the pastor called all the people together and told them to start planting around that water hole. He knew God would prosper those crops. He also knew that the crops belonging to the believers would be especially blessed, so when he parceled out the land, he interspersed the believers' plots among those of the unbelievers, so that the miracle of God could be clearly seen.

During that first season, everybody's crops flourished. Sinners' and believers' alike. Then the season for harvesting ended. All the sinners' crops died as usual. However, all of the believers' crops produced another harvest. Then another. Then another. The believers' crops just kept producing all year long!

Now you may say, "Brother Copeland, God did more than just prosper their souls. He worked miracles."

Yes, He did. But the miracles came as the result of a prospered soul. Because they believed His Word and were willing to listen to His voice, He revealed to them the secrets of success for their particular situation.

Deuteronomy 29:29 says this, "The secret things belong unto the Lord our God: but those things which are revealed belong unto us and to our children for ever, that we may do all the words of this law [or that we may put into practice the Word of God]."

How many times have you racked your brain, trying to figure out the solution to a problem? You *knew* there was an answer, but you just couldn't figure out what it was! In other words, the answer was a secret—a secret that only God knew. It was not revealed to you.

But, if you'd gone to the Word and really searched it in prayer and in meditation, that secret would have been revealed! God would have shown you precisely what the solution to that problem was.

In Mark 4:21-22, Jesus says, "Is a candle brought to be put under a bushel, or under a bed? and not to be set on a candlestick? For there is nothing hid, which shall not be manifested; neither was any thing kept secret, but that it should come abroad."

You see, God doesn't want you groping around in the dark. He wants to reveal His secrets to you. That's vital for you to understand. Once, when I was reading those verses, the Lord referred me to Proverbs 20:27. It says, "The spirit of man is the candle of the Lord...."

When I read that, the Lord spoke up on the inside of me. *Do you think I'd have a spirit born into this world just to put it under a bushel and keep it in darkness all of its life?* He asked. Instantly, I knew the answer. No! The only reason He brings human beings into this world is so that He can share His light with them.

That's why He's given us the Holy Spirit!

Do you have any idea what a tremendous resource the Holy Spirit is? Most believers don't. They get in church and say, "Oh yes, amen, brother. Thank God for the Holy Spirit. Praise God. Hallelujah." Then they go home and forget about Him.

It's not that they aren't sincere on Sunday. They are! They genuinely appreciate the little bit they understand about the Holy Spirit. But they haven't learned how to tap into the unlimited wisdom and power He can make available to them in their daily lives.

To give you an idea of just how important Jesus expected the Holy Spirit to be to us, look at John 16:6-7. There you'll find Jesus talking to His disciples about His coming death and departure from the Earth. He says, "Because I have said these things unto you, sorrow hath filled your heart. Nevertheless I tell you the truth; It is expedient for you that I go away: for if I go not away, the Comforter will not come unto you; but if I depart, I will send him unto you."

Can you imagine how the disciples must have reacted to that statement?

They probably wanted to say, "Lord, You must be kidding!

If you know Jesus Christ and are indwelt by the Holy Ghost, inside you is the answer to every financial problem, every spiritual problem and every physical problem that exists.

Nothing could possibly surpass what we've experienced with You. We've seen You raise the dead. We've seen You feed thousands with a few loaves and fishes. As long as You've been with us we've never lacked for anything. You're the One our people have been waiting on for hundreds and hundreds of years! How could it possibly be expedient for us for You to go away?"

Jesus answered that question in verse 13. "When he, the Spirit of truth, is come, he will guide you into all truth: for he shall not speak of himself; but whatsoever he shall hear, that shall he speak: and he will show you things to come."

Read that verse again and think about it.

Jesus said the Holy Spirit would guide us into *all* truth! Not just enough truth to get by. Not just an occasional truth to help us teach our Sunday school classes. All truth!

If you're a businessperson, that means the Holy Spirit will show you how to increase your profits and reduce your expenses. If you're a parent, it means the Holy Spirit will show you how to settle arguments between your kids. If you're a student, it means the Holy Spirit will show you how to excel in your classes.

In fact, if you know Jesus Christ and are indwelt by the Holy Ghost, inside you is the answer to every financial problem, every spiritual problem and every physical problem that exists. You already have answers to problems you don't even know about yet. The Word says that all the treasures of wisdom and knowledge are in Jesus. It also says *we* are in Christ Jesus and *He* is in us.

All it would take is just one God-given idea to change your life forever.

Can you begin to see now how God could prosper you?

There are so many people standing around wringing their hands and worrying. "God could never prosper me," they say. "All I get is this little paycheck. And my company's losing money so I know they won't give me a raise. How on earth can God prosper me?"

Maybe He'll give *you* the idea that will change your company's loss into a profit! Maybe He'll give you an idea for a new product and help you start your own company!

God has probably already given you more than one idea that would have made you rich if you'd have just recognized them. But you didn't even know they were there. Why not? Because you weren't paying attention to the things of God. You weren't seeking revelations of the "secret things." You were probably too busy watching television and listening to some announcer tell you which brand of toothpaste to buy or a newscaster trying to get you to join the recession!

Listen to me. The Holy Spirit can't help you or get through to you while your total attention is given to watching television. He's a gentleman. He just won't grab the remote control out of your hand and say, "Listen to me, dummy! I have some important things to tell you."

No, no. He'll just wait quietly for you to shut off all that other junk that's been occupying your mind and tune in to Him. Remember, James 4:8 says, "Draw nigh to God, and he will draw nigh to you...."

Right here is where most believers miss it. They're so involved in life, and even so involved in church activities and religious organizations, that they don't ever have any time to spend with the Lord. They never stop and fellowship with Him. All He gets is a few moments with them as they drive down the freeway—a few moments, maybe, during television commercials.

There are believers God has wanted to put into high political offices. He would have shown them how to solve some of this nation's problems. But He couldn't get their attention! So, He just left them where they were, spinning their wheels in a dead-end job. There are others God would have promoted until they became chief executives of major corporations, but they were too busy working toward their own little goals to find out His goals.

Don't miss out on God's plans of prosperity for you. Spend time with Him. Listen to Him and learn to recognize His voice.

It will take more than a couple of Bible verses and a five-minute prayer to tap in to the revelations the Holy Spirit has for you. You have to get serious about it.

If you think you don't have time to do that, think again.

How many hours a day do you spend in front of the television? How many hours a week do you spend reading the newspaper? How many hours do you spend reading novels and looking at magazines? How much time do you spend thinking about your problems?

Replace those things with the Word of God. Use that time to meditate on the Scriptures. Get in prayer and say, "Holy Spirit, I need to know what to do regarding this situation." Then listen. He'll start giving you the wisdom of God concerning your finances (or any other area of your life).

Will He really?

Sure He will! James 1:5-6 says, "If any of you lack wisdom,

let him ask of God, that giveth to all men liberally, and upbraid-
eth not; and it shall be given him. But let him ask in faith, nothing wavering. For he that wavereth is like a wave of the sea
driven with the wind and tossed."

Again though, let me warn you, we're talking about more
than reading a few quick scriptures a day and wishing for prosperity. We're talking about digging into the Word and staying
there until you begin to hear from the Holy Spirit and until you
develop a faith that doesn't waver.

That doesn't happen overnight.

Like a spiritual farmer, you have to plant and weed and water
the Word within you. It will take some time, effort and patience,
but I promise you, the harvest will be well worth the wait.

The Seeds of Your Success

If, by chance, you were hoping to discover a fast and easy
formula for prosperity, you probably know by now you won't
find it here.

God's principles of prosperity work. They work anywhere,
any time, for anyone. But they're not easy and the results certainly aren't instant.

To truly live by these principles, you will have to develop
spiritually as you never have before. Notice, I didn't say you
would have to "grow," I said you would have to develop.
There's a difference. Growth comes easily, almost automatically
to the healthy believer. But development is tougher. Development takes work.

Like the bodybuilder, you have to put some pressure on
your spiritual muscles. You have to exercise your faith. You
have to accept the fact that real development takes time.

A man came up to me once and said, "Man, your ministry
just took off overnight, didn't it?"

"If it did," I answered, "it was certainly the longest night I ever spent in my life!"

From his perspective our success did seem to spring up quickly. That's because he didn't see me during all those hours and weeks and months and years I spent in the Word of God. He didn't see all the commitment and determination behind that success. He just saw the results.

So, right now, I want to take you behind the scenes and let you in on the secrets God began to teach me more than 41 years ago. I want to show you how to go to the Word of God for a faith workout that will put the promise of prosperity—and every other promise of God—within your reach.

Don't Just Sit There, Start Planting!

Thus far, we've focused on God's part of the plan of prosperity. We've talked about His will, His why and His way. But there has to be more, right? There has to be something you and I can do to put His plan into action in our lives.

There is. In fact, that "something" is the key to the very treasure house of God. Ignore it and you'll never be able to open the door to God's prosperity. Use it, and nothing in the world will be able to keep you out.

Look at what the Lord says in Joshua 1:7-8 and you'll see what I'm talking about.

Be thou strong and very courageous, that thou mayest observe to do according to all the law, which Moses my servant commanded thee: turn not from it to the right hand or to the left, that thou mayest prosper whithersoever thou goest. This book of the law shall not depart out of thy mouth; but thou shalt meditate therein day and night, that thou mayest observe to do according to all that is written therein: for then thou shalt make thy way prosperous, and then thou shalt have good success.

> When it comes to prosperity, the Word of God is the secret to your success.

When that passage was written, "the law" was the only written record of God's Word. So, let's read that last verse again substituting "the Word of God" for "the law."

"[The Word of God] shall not depart out of thy mouth; but thou shalt meditate therein day and night, that thou mayest observe to do according to all that is written therein: for then thou shalt make thy way prosperous, and then thou shalt have good success."

Deuteronomy 29:9 says essentially the same thing: "Keep therefore the words of this covenant, and do them, that ye may prosper in all that ye do."

In short, what these verses are saying is this: When it comes to prosperity, the Word of God is the secret to your success.

I can just hear the wheels turning in your mind. "Wait a minute!" you say. "I know plenty of people who read the Bible and it's not making them prosperous!"

You're exactly right. That's why God didn't tell Joshua to "read" the Word of God. He told him that he should:

1. Continually speak....
2. Meditate....
3. Observe to do....

You may know a whole church full of poor folks who are reading the Word of God, but I dare say you don't know one single person who's following those three steps and staying poor at the same time. It just can't be done!

The sad fact is you may not know anyone who's following those three steps *at all!* Most believers are content just to scan a few scriptures before bed each night and to follow along in their Bibles as the pastor reads on Sunday. But that kind of dabbling will never open the doors of God's treasure house! If you really want to prosper, you'll have to be much more extreme about the Word than that.

"Extreme? Oh no. I don't believe in being an extremist!"

Well, if you want to have God's kind of success, you'd better start believing in it. God certainly does—especially where His Word is concerned. Take a look, for example, at what He told the Israelite people to do in Deuteronomy 6:6-9:

> These words, which I command thee this day, shall be in thine heart: And thou shalt teach them diligently unto thy children, and shalt talk of them when thou sittest in thine house, and when thou walkest by the way, and when thou liest down, and when thou risest up. And thou shalt bind them for a sign upon thine hand, and they shall be as frontlets between thine eyes. And thou shalt write them upon the posts of thy house, and on thy gates.

God didn't tell those people to watch four or five hours of soap operas and talk about the weather. He didn't even tell them to spend a reasonable amount of time in the Word each day. He told them to keep their attention on the Word at all times. Later, Solomon said it again in Proverbs 4:21 when he wrote, "Let them [My Words] not depart from thine eyes; keep them in the midst of thine heart."

Any way you look at it, that's extreme!

Why would God tell us to do anything that extreme? Because He knows how much power lies within His Word.

You see, the Word of God is more than just a collection of divinely inspired promises. It literally carries within it the power to make those promises become a reality in your life. That's why the poorest street bum in the world can prosper when he gets hold of the Word of God. Regardless of his lack of education, regardless of his lack of resources, regardless of his lack of opportunities, the Word itself can make him prosperous because it's packed with the supernatural power of God.

Just think about that! Every promise in the Word of God contains the power to fulfill itself. All you have to do to get the Word to release that power is plant it by faith within your heart. Put it in your mouth and then do it.

Is it tough for you to believe such a thing is possible?

It shouldn't be. You see it happen in the natural world all the time.

If, for example, I were to put a tomato seed into your hand and tell you that within that tiny, dry seed lies the power to produce a stalk thousands of times bigger than the seed, to produce leaves, roots and round, red tomatoes, you wouldn't have any trouble believing that, would you? You know from experience that even though that scrawny seed doesn't look like a tomato factory, somehow, given the right environment, it will become one.

Jesus says the Word of God works by that same principle. There is miraculous power within it. It is a seed that, once planted by faith in a human heart, will produce more blessings than you can imagine. Prosperity is just one of them. There are many, such as:

THE NEW BIRTH: First Peter 1:23 says we are "born again, not of corruptible seed, but of incorruptible, by the word of God, which liveth and abideth for ever."

SPIRITUAL GROWTH: First Peter 2:2 says spiritual growth comes from the Word. "As newborn babes, desire the sincere milk of the word, that ye may grow thereby."

FREEDOM: Jesus said, "...If ye continue in my word, then are ye my disciples indeed; And ye shall know the truth, and the truth shall make you free" (John 8:31-32).

HEALING: "My son, attend to my words; incline thine ear unto my sayings. Let them not depart from thine eyes; keep them in the midst of thine heart. For they are life unto those that find them, and health to all their flesh" (Proverbs 4:20-22).

PROSPERITY: We've already read this verse once, but let's read it again. "...Meditate therein [in My Word] day and night, that thou mayest observe to do according to all that is written therein: for then thou shalt make thy way prosperous, and then thou shalt have good success" (Joshua 1:8).

Those are just a few things the Word of God has the power to produce in your life. The list could go on and on. In fact, through the Word, you have access to everything you need for life and godliness. Second Peter 1:3-4 says,

His divine power hath given unto us all things that pertain unto life and godliness, through the knowledge of him that hath called us to glory and virtue: Whereby are given unto us exceeding great and precious promises: that by these ye might be partakers of the divine nature, having escaped the corruption that is in the world through lust.

Great and precious promises! Promises that contain the power to produce everything you need. Once you truly begin to grasp that, you *will* become extreme about the Word of God. That's what happened to me.

Back in 1967, I caught a glimpse of what the Word of God could do. I caught a glimpse of the power within it and I became extreme about it. Before long, I had a Bible in every room of my house, a Bible in my car and a tape player going nearly all the time.

I spent every possible moment in the Word of God because I wanted the power of that Word inside me more than I wanted anything else in the world. I knew it would blow the limits off my life, limits that had held me back and kept me down for years.

From that time on, when I read the Word of God, I wasn't just reading, I was planting seeds—seeds of prosperity, seeds of health, seeds of protection and seeds of victory for every area of my life.

If you truly want to enjoy the prosperity the Word of God promises, you'll have to do that too. You'll have to plant and plant and plant. You'll have to read the Word and speak the Word and meditate on the Word.

Meditate?

Yes, meditate.

DIGGING DEEPER

4

Chapter 4
Digging Deeper

Sadly enough, very few believers today really know how to "plant" the Word deeply within themselves. They know how to read it. They know how to listen to preachers preach it. They know how to get together and talk about it. Many of them faithfully do all those things. Yet all too often the Word still doesn't take root in their hearts. So, their lives remain unchanged.

The problem is, they've failed to follow the second step God gave to Joshua. They've failed to *meditate* on the Word.

Meditation simply means thinking about the Word, reflecting on it, and praying about it until it begins to burn itself into your mind and your heart. It means pondering a particular scripture and mentally applying it to your own circumstances until it permanently marks your consciousness.

Meditation is a profoundly effective process. The Scriptures prove it.

Take the story of Abram, for example. When he received the word of God telling him that he was going to have a son, he was an old man. His wife, Sarai, was also old, well past the age of childbearing. What's more, she had been barren all her life.

In their minds, Abram and Sarai saw themselves as an aging, childless couple. Over the years that image had been imbedded deeply within them. They had totally given up any other hope. In fact Abram had already made plans to leave his estate to his servant Eliezar of Damascus. When the Lord spoke to Abram and told him He was going to give him and Sarai a child, Abram could hardly imagine such a thing. That's why God didn't just make Abram a verbal promise and leave it at that. He did something else. Let's look at Genesis 15:5-6 and see what it was: "And he [God] brought him [Abram] forth abroad, and said, Look now toward heaven, and tell the stars, if thou be able to number them: and he said unto him, So shall thy seed be. And he [Abram] believed...."

God didn't just leave Abram with his old image of himself as a barren old man. He gave him a new image to ponder, an image of God's promise being fulfilled.

Can't you just see Abram staring out at the stars, trying to count them? Looking into the sparkling light of one after another and visualizing the faces of his grandchildren and great-grandchildren? Filling the eyes of his heart with the promise of God?

A few years later, when that vision was growing dim (and after Abram and Sarai had tried to help God's plan along by bringing Sarai's maidservant Hagar into the picture), God spoke again. Once again, He did something that would mark the minds of Abram and Sarai forever. He gave them new names.

> Neither shall thy name any more be called Abram, but thy name shall be Abraham; for a father of many nations have I made thee.... And God said unto Abraham, As for Sarai thy wife, thou shalt not call her name Sarai, but Sarah shall her name be. And I will bless her, and give thee a son also of her: yea, I will bless her, and she shall be a mother of nations; kings of people shall be of her (Genesis 17:5, 15-16).

God made sure that His promise to Abraham and Sarah became more than words to be heard and forgotten. He arranged it so that every day, countless times each day, whenever they heard or called each other's name, the promise of God would again come to mind. They would never again be able to separate themselves from it. It became a permanent part of their identity.

That is meditation in its most perfect form. As a believer, it's one of the most powerful tools you have.

Use it.

If you're trying to plant God's Word about prosperity in your heart, begin to visualize those prosperity promises coming to pass in your life. Replace the old impoverished images you have of yourself. Make them match what the Word of God says instead. See yourself with the answer instead of the problem.

Replace the old, impoverished images you have of yourself. Make them match what the Word of God says, instead.

If, for example, you've never had enough money to help the poor, go to 2 Corinthians 9:8 and read God's promise about that: "And God is able to make all grace abound toward you; that ye, always having all sufficiency in all things, may abound to every good work."

Think about that promise. See yourself being able to write a $5,000 check and giving it to an organization that feeds hungry children. Immediately begin to act on that image. Whenever you sense the Spirit leading you to give, give whatever you can. It may not be much at first, but don't worry about that. Just keep developing that image inside you. See yourself giving more. In your mind, practice writing those checks again and again.

Soon faith will start to rise up inside you. The promise of God will begin to get real inside you. *I know it's mine,* you'll think. *God is making all grace abound toward me and I will have all sufficiency in all things. Hallelujah, I will abound to every good work!*

"Brother Copeland, surely you're not saying I should use

my *imagination!*"

Yes, that's precisely what I'm saying. Why do you think God gave it to you? Coupled with the Word of God, your imagination is a tremendous thing. Let it help you visualize God's promise. A hazy hope is not enough. You need a detailed picture!

I first learned how to use my imagination that way as a kicker for my high school football team. I'd lie in bed and visualize myself making the kick. I could see the turf beneath my feet, the laces on the ball and the goal posts in front of me. Then, in my mind's eye, I would visualize the football sailing between the posts. I'd do that over and over, building an image of that successful kick within me.

Let me warn you though, sometimes it's difficult to create such new images—especially when old images are blocking the way. If, for example, you've been living on the edge of financial disaster since you were in kindergarten, it will take a lot of time in prayer and in the Word to change the picture of poverty that's been established within you.

Years ago, when I was many, many pounds overweight, I read countless books on weight loss. One thing almost all of them said was this: "See yourself slim."

I tried. Believe me, I tried! But I just couldn't do it. Every time I shut my eyes I saw that same fat guy I'd seen reflected in the mirror 10 minutes before. Even when I succeeded in losing some weight, that inner image didn't change. So, I'd end up putting the weight right back on again.

I finally went on a fast, meditating on the Word of God and staying in prayer, until I overcame that image.

Why is it so hard to change those old mental images of ourselves? Because we've spent years developing them. They're firmly entrenched in our minds. But regardless of how tough it may be, if we ever want to enjoy the blessings God has for us, we must do something about them.

We're going to have to follow the instructions of God and "be not conformed to this world: but be ye transformed by the renewing of your mind..." (Romans 12:2), and "Casting down imaginations, and every high thing that exalteth itself against the knowledge of God, and bringing into captivity every thought to the obedience of Christ" (2 Corinthians 10:5).

Quite often when I talk about building an inner image with the Word of God, I find believers are wary of such things. They say it sounds like positive thinking or New Age techniques. No, New Age, etc., sounds like this!

Well, where do you think the devil got those things? You don't think he ever came up with anything on his own, do you? Of course not! He's a thief. He stole that passage about meditation from the first chapter of Joshua, took out the part about the Word of God and gave it to some folks who were foolish enough to fall for it.

Don't shy away from meditation just because the devil has a counterfeit of it. The very fact that he's tried to duplicate it indicates just how powerful it is!

Instead of the phrase "building an inner image with the promises of God" I could have just said "building real Bible hope with the promises of God" because that's what it is. You now, however, know that real Bible hope takes the form of an image on the inside of you, and faith is the substance of that image (hope).

There is nothing wrong with meditation as long as you meditate the right thing. THE WORD OF GOD IS THE RIGHT THING! Put the powerful art of meditation to work for you. Use it to plant the Word of God deeply into your heart and mind. Then, once that Word is planted, do everything you can to protect your crop.

5

HOW TO PREVENT CROP FAILURES

Chapter 5
How to Prevent Crop Failures

Does simply planting the Word of God in your heart guarantee that you will have a harvest?

No, it doesn't.

Once you plant, you must constantly be alert and on guard against certain elements—elements that, left unchecked, can cause a spiritual crop failure. Jesus, Himself, warned us about them in one of the greatest parables He ever told. So let's go to Mark 4:14-25 and read that parable:

> The sower soweth the word. And these are they by the way side, where the word is sown; but when they have heard, Satan cometh immediately, and taketh away the word that was sown in their hearts. And these are they likewise which are sown on stony ground; who, when they have heard the word, immediately receive it with gladness; And have no root in themselves, and so endure but for a time: afterward, when affliction or persecution ariseth for the word's sake, immediately they are offended. And these are they which are sown among thorns; such as hear the word, And the cares of this world, and the deceitfulness of riches, and the lusts of others things entering in, choke the word, and it becometh unfruitful. And these are they which are sown on good ground; such as hear the word, and receive it, and bring forth fruit, some thirtyfold, some sixty, and some an hundred.... Take heed what ye hear: with what measure ye mete, it shall be measured to you: and unto you that hear shall more be given. For he that hath, to

him shall be given: and he that hath not, from him shall be taken even that which he hath.

What a marvelous parable that is! I actually believe it's the most important parable Jesus ever told. Why? Because, when the principle it teaches is understood and applied, it will work in every part of our lives—spiritual, physical, mental and financial.

Jesus, Himself, alluded to that before He told it by saying, "Know ye not this parable? and how then will ye know all parables?" (Mark 4:13). In other words, He was telling His disciples, "Boys, this is the granddaddy of them all. Understand this one, and you'll begin to see how the kingdom of God operates."

Since we're concentrating on the subject of prosperity right now, however, let's narrow our focus and go through the parable again verse by verse and see how it applies to that specific area.

By the Wayside

"And these are they by the way side, where the word is sown; but when they have heard, Satan cometh immediately, and taketh away the word that was sown in their hearts" (Mark 4:15).

It's interesting to note that in this parable, as in others, Jesus doesn't even refer to those who refuse to hear the Word or to those who, upon hearing it, reject it. Obviously, He expects us to take time to listen to the Word. He expects us to receive it. He has nothing at all to say to those who don't.

You, however, *are* a "hearer." As you've read this book, the Word has been sown in your heart. You've heard, for example, that "God takes pleasure in the prosperity of His servant." The question is, now that the Word is there within you, what will you do with it?

Will you be like those by the wayside who let Satan come and steal the Word that was sown? Will you entertain doubts?

Hmm. I don't know about that verse I read. I know it says God takes pleasure in the prosperity of His servants, but I've sure seen a lot of people at church who are having financial problems. They're good people too! No, I'm not too sure about that verse after all. It must not mean what I thought it meant.

If the devil can get you to think like that for a little while, he'll be able to steal that Word right out of your heart, and it will never do you any good.

Stony Ground

"And these are they likewise which are sown on stony ground; who, when they have heard the word, immediately receive it with gladness; And have no root in themselves, and so endure but for a time: afterward, when affliction or persecution ariseth for the word's sake, immediately they are offended" (Mark 4:16-17).

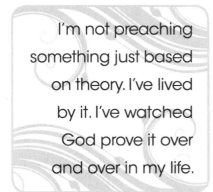

I'm not preaching something just based on theory. I've lived by it. I've watched God prove it over and over in my life.

After more than 42 years of experience in the ministry, I'd say this is the category into which most Christians fall. Initially, they get excited about the Word of God. "Praise the Lord! Hallelujah. God takes delight in the prosperity of His servants!" they say. But then, somehow, things just don't work out like they thought.

Their bank balance doesn't double overnight. They go through some disappointments. They suffer some criticism. Before you know it, they become offended at the Word.

Of course, most of them won't be honest enough to admit that they are offended at the Word. They'll start getting huffy about the preacher who preached it to them instead.

I never could understand that. Countless people have become angry with me for preaching what the Word of God says about prosperity. Why do they become offended at *me?* I didn't write the Bible! I wish I had written it, but I didn't. On top of that, I'm not preaching something just based on theory. I've lived by it. I've watched God prove it over and over in my life.

But invariably, I'll preach about it and someone will get upset with me. "It didn't work for me!" they'll say.

Listen, if that happens to you, don't get offended. Go to God with it and find out why it's not working for you. Let Him show you where the problem is.

If you let the devil cause you to get crosswise with me or with anybody else in the Body of Christ, he'll be able to steal the Word from your heart. He'll pull the plug right out of you and drain the Word like water from a bucket.

The moment you catch yourself becoming offended say, *"Oh no you don't.* You're not stealing the Word out of me, you lying devil." Then get right down on your knees and repent before God.

If you search the Word and listen to the Spirit within you and still feel you've been given inaccurate information, pray for the one who gave it to you! Don't get offended. Taking offense never comes from God. He says we're to be rooted and grounded in love. So, reject those feelings of offense and give yourself to that person in love and in prayer.

Now, let's take another look at this particular verse and see what it says about persecution and affliction. "...Afterward, when affliction or persecution ariseth for the word's sake, immediately they are offended" (verse 17).

Here's the first thing I want you to notice about that phrase. It says that persecution comes "for the Word's sake." Despite what you may think, the devil doesn't persecute you because you're anybody special. He persecutes you because once you have the Word in your heart, you're a threat to him. He persecutes you in an effort to keep that Word from becoming fruitful.

Here's the second thing I want you to notice about that phrase. It doesn't say "'If' affliction or persecution arises," it says "when" it arises. I'm warning you right now, just like Jesus did, if you start digging around in the Word this way, you will run into trouble.

Somebody is always accusing faith preachers of telling folks that if they'll just believe God, they'll never have any more problems. Well, I've never heard anybody preach that, and nobody with any brains at all ever would. It's just not so.

Everyone I've ever known who decided to live by faith usually was handed more problems than they'd ever had in their lives. (Of course, they also had more answers!) You won't be any different. If you let the Word of God concerning prosperity get down in your heart, you will learn more about the devil than you ever wanted to know, because he will try to mess you up every time you turn around.

Financially, he's been lording it over the Body of Christ for years. (He's always known the money belonged to God, but as long as we didn't know it, he could pretty well do as he pleased with it.) He's had a slick operation going, and he won't give it up without a fight. So, you might as well expect him to come after you.

But, thank God, through Christ Jesus you have the power to defeat him. When he brings problems your way, you don't have to lie down and let them roll over you. Just keep the faith and keep fighting the devil until you win. Act on the Word and resist the devil (stand firm against him) and he will flee from you!

Sure you'll get knocked down sometimes. But when you do just get back up and say, "Look here, devil, I'm playing until I win! I'm not letting you steal the Word out of my heart. It's in there and I'm going to meditate on it, and I'm going to say it with my mouth, and I'm going to act on it until God's blessings overtake me. If you don't believe it, just hide and watch!"

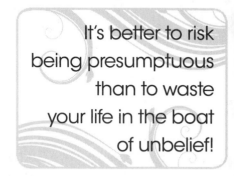

It's better to risk being presumptuous than to waste your life in the boat of unbelief!

If you'll take that attitude, God will not only help you solve the problems the devil brings your way, He will help you solve the ones you create yourself. He's done that for me. There have been times when I thought I was stepping out in faith, only to realize later I'd stepped out in presumption and landed myself in a situation I shouldn't have.

When I went to the Lord to find out what I should do, He just said, *Stay on the Word, son. Together we'll overcome this thing. And don't be that kind of fellow anymore.*

If you act on the Word out of the sincerity of your heart and if you'll steadfastly stay with the Word, Jesus will never let you down—no matter how many dumb mistakes you make. He proved that the night Peter jumped out of the boat in the middle of the lake.

Have you ever stopped to think about that incident? Peter hadn't been praying or seeking God's will before he did that. On impulse he just blurted out, "Lord, if it's You, bid me come."

What was Jesus supposed to say? He couldn't very well say,

"It's not Me." I suppose He could have said, "Wait a minute, you turkey. You don't have the faith to get out here. You'd better stay in that boat or you'll drown for sure."

But He didn't say that to Peter—and He won't say it to you. If you want to get out and walk by faith, He'll get out there with you and pick you up when you start sinking. He'll walk you back to the boat if necessary.

For some reason, when we think of that incident we always think about Peter starting to doubt. We always think of him slipping down in the waves. And he did. But you know what? He also walked on the water for a while. None of the others did that.

It's better to risk being presumptuous than to waste your life in the boat of unbelief! If you have to, just dive into the water and say, "My God, I'm sinking." He will be there to rescue you.

Step out of the boat! Yes, the devil will persecute you and afflict you, but in Jesus you're more than a match for him. If he comes at you a hundred times harder than ever before, get a hundred times tougher.

Don't sit around whining about it either. Take it as a compliment. Heavy duty persecution means you've made it to the big league. It means the devil is taking you so seriously that he's sending in his best players in an effort to get you out of the game!

The players who make it to the Super Bowl don't look for some way out of it, do they? They don't say, "Boy, I sure wish I didn't have to play in that Super Bowl. Those guys are the biggest, toughest players in the country. Maybe I'll get sick and I won't have to play."

No! They relish the opportunity! "Let me at 'em," they say. "I've worked all my life to get here, and now I'll prove I'm a winner!"

That's the way God approaches things—from a position of power. He never stops and wonders if He will have enough resources to get poor little you over your problems this time. He knows He can beat anything the devil brings against you. Trust Him and say with the Apostle Paul:

...I will all the more gladly glory in my weaknesses and infirmities, that the strength and power of Christ, the Messiah, may rest—yes, may pitch a tent [over] and dwell—upon me! So for the sake of Christ, I am well pleased and take pleasure in infirmities, insults, hardships, persecutions, perplexities and distresses; for when I am weak (in human strength), then am I [truly] strong—able, powerful in divine strength (2 Corinthians 12:9-10, *The Amplified Bible*).

Among Thorns

"And these are they which are sown among thorns; such as hear the word, And the cares of this world, and the deceitfulness of riches, and the lusts of other things entering in, choke the word, and it becometh unfruitful" (Mark 4:18-19).

So now you've heard the Word of God concerning prosperity. You've received it. You've put doubts out of your mind. You've made it through some persecutions and afflictions. And you've refused to let the devil steal the Word from your heart.

What do you think he'll do next?

He'll try to smother the Word with cares before it can grow. That word "care" is a word that literally means anxiety, concern, an overwhelming mental oppression. The most familiar word we have for it is "worry."

You'll pick up the newspaper and find out that the stock market has hit an all-time low. You'll turn on the television and hear some newscaster predicting recession or depression. Your neighbor will drop by and tell you about a friend of his who just got laid off his job.

What will happen to the Word of God that's been planted in your heart then? Will you say, "Well, praise God, no matter what anybody says, God takes pleasure in the prosperity of His servant and He never changes, so I'm expecting Him to prosper me in spite of it all!"? Or, will you start worrying and let that worry choke the Word?

If you start trusting God in the area of prosperity, the devil will see to it that you'll have no shortage of bad news, ever. He'll come at you through the radio, through the television, through your relatives, through the newspaper. He'll just stuff you full of the cares of the world if you'll let him. So don't let him. When the going gets tough, tune out the world and tune into the Word, and you'll pass through just fine.

THE LAW OF INCREASE

Chapter 6
The Law of Increase

The verses we will look at now are two of the most crucial you'll ever read. They capture a law that governs everything in the kingdom of God. Everything. Until you begin to understand that law, you will never be able to have real spiritual success—in the area of prosperity or anywhere else.

"Take heed what ye hear: with what measure ye mete, it shall be measured to you: and unto you that hear shall more be given. For he that hath, to him shall be given: and he that hath not, from him shall be taken even that which he hath" (Mark 4:24-25).

I call that the Law of Increase. Before you can really understand it, you first have to realize that when Jesus said the word "hear" in that passage, He wasn't simply referring to the vibrations that bounce around on your eardrums. He was talking about something much more significant.

You see, we don't really hear with our ears. We hear with our minds. We hear with our hearts. You can line up 10 people and say the same thing to all of them, and each one will come away with a different meaning. Each person will take the words he heard with his ears, mix them with his own personal interpretations and reactions, and come up with something unique.

For example, when my children were small, someone might have said to me, "Kenneth, your son, John, is standing out in the street." Now, that person has painted a simple verbal picture for me. It's a picture of little John standing in the street.

But I might get hold of it and add a car to it. Not just any car either, but a car with a madman behind the wheel driving 100 miles an hour. If I've been walking around with a lot of fear in my heart, I might even visualize John flying up in the air, blood everywhere.

Now all this guy said to me was, "John's in the street." But I heard something much worse. I took the fears and the thoughts that were in my mind, added them in and came up with a tragedy.

I can preach to you about prosperity all day long, but if you take the Word and measure it with skepticism and doubt, you still won't prosper.

On the other hand, if I'd been filling my ears and my heart with the Word of God for years, I'd probably hear something entirely different. Instead of hearing tragedy, I'd start praising God for His promises of protection. Instead of worrying, I'd start praying. "Lord, I thank You that You've promised You'll be with John in time of trouble. Thank You that You will satisfy him with long life because he has honored his father and mother, which is the first commandment with promise."

Can you see the difference? In one instance, my heart heard fear. In the other, my heart heard faith. In both cases, my physical ears played only a minimal part.

"Be careful how you hear," Jesus said. "Because when I deal with you, I will be using your measuring stick, not Mine. However you measure it is how it will be measured back to you."

I can preach to you about prosperity all day long, but if you take the Word and measure it with skepticism and doubt, you still won't prosper.

Two people can hear the same Word. One will measure it with faith. "God has pleasure in the prosperity of His servant.

Hallelujah!" he says. "I believe that with all my heart, and I'll keep on believing it until I receive that prosperity."

The other will say, "I don't care what Bible verses he comes up with, I just don't trust old Copeland. I'll give this prosperity stuff a try, but I doubt very much if anything will come of it. It's just too good to be true."

Both those people will receive exactly what they expect. God will measure to them just as they measured the Word. One will prosper—the other won't. Do you want to know something funny? The skeptic will take the fact that he didn't prosper and use it to prove he was right all along. "I told you it wouldn't work and, sure enough, it didn't!"

Once you begin to understand the Law of Increase, you'll also begin to better understand what Jesus said earlier in the Parable of the Sower about the thirtyfold, sixtyfold and hundredfold return. Let's look back at that scripture for a moment.

"And these are they which are sown on good ground; such as hear the word, and receive it, and bring forth fruit, some thirty-fold, some sixty, and some an hundred" (Mark 4:20).

Why is it some receive one kind of return, some another? Does God just arbitrarily give greater blessings to one person than He gives to someone else?

No! He measures the blessings back to us according to the way we measure the Word. If we measure it with a hundredfold measure, we'll get a hundredfold blessing.

I like the way *The Amplified Bible* puts it. It says, "Be careful what you are hearing. The measure [of thought and study] you give [to the truth you hear] will be the measure [of virtue and knowledge] that comes back to you..." (Mark 4:24).

Your prosperity depends on how much thought and study and attention you give God's Word in that area. Are you willing to give that Word first place in your heart? Are you willing to receive it in faith instead of with skepticism? Are you willing to defend it, to fight the devil when he tries to steal it? The bottom line is, just how serious are you about God's Word? Is it final authority in your life?

The way you measure or esteem the Word will determine the way you receive the fruit of the Word. What will you do when the deceitfulness of riches and the lusts of other things start weighing on you? Will you hang in there and keep on believing the Word when people start calling you an extremist? Or when they start accusing you of being financially greedy? Will you continue to measure the Word with faith, or will you back off?

"Now Brother Copeland," you may say, "you know there are folks who have taken this message so far they've moved out of the will of God. What about them?"

It's not our business to judge them. Those people are not our servants. If you start judging them, you'll be just as far out of the will of God as they are. So just quit worrying about them.

The truth is, if Jesus Christ of Nazareth showed up in the flesh, all the religious folks today would instantly brand Him as an extremist, a fanatic just like they did in His day. He couldn't be a member in good standing of any denomination I know. So, you'd be wise not to throw labels like that around. Just leave the judging to God, OK?

For your own protection, however, let me say this: You become an extremist when you try to use your faith to acquire things the Word of God doesn't promise you. That's dangerous ground.

If, for example, you announced one day that by faith you were claiming every oil well in the world as your own, you'd be totally off base. The Bible never promised you every oil well in the world. And remember, you must have the faith to back up what you desire, and faith has to be based on the Word. You cannot receive beyond what you believe. You cannot believe beyond the Word that you have stored in your heart. "With the heart man believeth..." (Romans 10:10).

That is the reason you need to find out what the Word says about what you desire and stand securely in faith on the promises of God.

> Gloria and I saw that there was power and deliverance in the Word and that the more we fed our spirits with the Word, the stronger our faith would grow.

Now, when I say that, some will become disappointed even though the Bible contains thousands of promises that cover every need imaginable. "You mean that's all I get?" they'll say. "Just what's written in the Bible?"

Others will be thrilled. "Wow! Praise God! Everything in that Book is mine!" They'll measure it differently and they'll receive it in exactly the way they measured it.

I'll warn you though, sometimes you might have a struggle to measure the Word with faith and joy when you first hear it. When I first started hearing what the Word had to say about finances, I was $22,000 in debt. I don't mean I was just behind on current bills. Those debts were all outstanding. Most of my creditors never expected a dime from me.

Right in the middle of that situation, Gloria and I caught hold of the Word. We saw that there was power in the Word. We saw that deliverance was in the Word. And somehow God helped us understand that the more we fed our spirit the Word, the stronger our faith would grow.

So we made a decision. We set our hearts to be obedient to the Word. We agreed that we would take every truth we saw there and apply it in our lives—whether we felt like it or not.

Not long after that, we ran into a scripture that said, "Owe no man any thing, but to love one another..." (Romans 13:8). That hit me hard. I said, "Oh God, surely You're not telling me not to ever borrow money. Please, don't tell me that! You're already speaking to me about a worldwide ministry, and now You're coming around telling me not to borrow any money? Those two just don't mix!"

I even ran and got *The Amplified Bible* in hopes that it would translate that verse differently. You know what it said? "Keep out of debt...." That left me in worse trouble than ever.

Believe me, at first I had a tough time measuring that scripture to my advantage. *I've had it either way I go,* I thought. *I'm hung if I do and I'm hung if I don't. If I don't borrow the money, I'll never be able to do what God has instructed me to do in worldwide ministry. If I do borrow the money, I'll be out of His will. What will I do?*

I was in a real quandary about it for a while.

Then Gloria and I talked about it and we came to an agreement. "We can't turn back now," we said. "We've made a quality decision and we won't retreat from it. We'll stick with the Word of God no matter what. We'll believe that somehow it will turn out to our advantage."

I didn't know enough back then to understand how it could turn out to our advantage. I just knew enough about the nature of God and the nature of His Word to know that it would. Quite honestly, I didn't choose to obey that scripture because I thought it would make me prosperous. If I had been looking for wealth, I would have looked somewhere else. I put that scripture into action in my life strictly because that's what God told me to do.

But I wasn't the only one having a real struggle. It was

difficult for Gloria to measure it to her advantage too. We were living in a terrible little house at the time. (Just to give you an idea of how bad it was, they eventually tore down the whole block right up to our house.) She wanted a new home more than just about any natural thing.

How could we ever buy a decent house without borrowing? It didn't seem possible. So, to her, it was as if that scripture had said, "Gloria, you can't have a new house."

But she refused to measure it that way. She grabbed the devil by the throat and said, "Look here now, you're not cheating me out of my house." Then she started believing that somehow God could provide her with a debt-free house, even though in her own mind she couldn't understand how that could happen.

Now, after more than 42 years, we can look back and see that trusting God instead of borrowing has been the greatest financial decision we've ever made. We can see how God paid off that $22,000 debt I owed, how He financed the ministry, how He provided the home of our choice, how He met every need and fulfilled every desire of our hearts. Now it's easier to read, Owe no man anything but to love him, and measure it with faith and with joy.

But it wasn't always that easy—and it won't be easy for you, especially when the Word has just been freshly planted in your heart.

Look again at what *The Amplified Bible* says, "...The measure [of thought and study] you give [to the truth you hear] will be the measure...that comes back to you..." (Mark 4:24). If you want to ensure yourself a thirtyfold, sixtyfold or even a hundredfold return, you will have to give the Word a tremendous amount of thought and study!

One of the reasons Gloria and I have seen such marvelous

results in our lives and in our ministry is because when we realized what the Word of God would do, we literally immersed ourselves in it. In those early days of becoming established in God's Word, we looked around and realized that the world was coming at us from every direction. Every time we turned on the radio or the television or picked up a newspaper, we were hearing what the voices of the world had to say. So we just tuned out the world and tuned in to the Word of God instead.

It wasn't that we quit those things, we just didn't have time for them anymore. For many months we spent nearly every waking moment either reading the Word, listening to tapes on the Word or thinking about the Word.

All that time in the Word eventually had a powerful effect on us. As Romans 10:17 says, "Faith cometh by hearing, and hearing by the word of God." So we grew stronger and stronger in faith. And as that happened, we were able to increase the size of our measure!

The same thing will happen to you if you'll devote yourself to the Word. By the way, we still have to attend to God's Word if we want to continue in victory. This is a lifetime proposition.

There are a great many believers who start out devoting themselves to the Word, but they make the mistake of expecting instant, miraculous results. When that doesn't happen, they're disappointed. Don't do that.

Jesus once said, "...Man shall not live by bread alone, but by every word that proceedeth out of the mouth of God" (Matthew 4:4). In other words, the Word of God feeds the spirit man just as bread feeds the body. Food has to be built into your body. The vitamins and minerals it contains have a cumulative effect on it, don't they? In fact, almost anything that affects your body instantaneously is considered dangerous.

Much the same thing is true with the Word of God. It has a

cumulative effect. Yes, at times God will act instantly and perform a miracle, but only to get things back on track. His real intention is for you to feed on His Word, to grow in strength and in faith, and to bear fruit in due season.

So don't be in such a hurry. Stay in the Word. Be patient and the results will come.

7

DEBT

Chapter 7
Debt

Unless I miss my guess, some of you who are reading this book won't be able to concentrate on another thing I say until we deal with the issue of debt that I brought up in the last chapter.

Your mind is going off in every direction. *Is he saying it's a sin to borrow money? Oh my goodness, I'll never get by without borrowing money! My church even borrows money—surely my church can't be wrong!* Et cetera, et cetera.

First of all let me assure you, I didn't say it was a sin for you to borrow money. I didn't say it was not a sin either. That's for you and God to determine.

As you seek His will on the matter, however, be sure to seriously consider what He's already said about the subject in His Word. For example:

Keep out of debt and owe no man anything, except to love one another... (Romans 13:8, *The Amplified Bible).*

When the Lord your God blesses you as He promised you, then you shall lend to many nations, but you shall not borrow; and you shall rule over many nations, but they shall not rule over you (Deuteronomy 15:6, *The Amplified Bible).*

The Lord shall open unto thee his good treasure, the heaven to give the rain unto thy land in his season, and to bless all the work of thine hand: and thou shalt lend unto many nations, and thou shalt not borrow. And the Lord shall make thee the head, and not the tail; and thou shalt be above only, and thou shalt not be beneath; if that thou hearken unto the commandments of the Lord thy God, which I command thee this day, to observe and to do them (Deuteronomy 28:12-13).

...The borrower is servant to the lender (Proverbs 22:7).

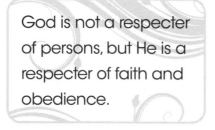

God is not a respecter of persons, but He is a respecter of faith and obedience.

It seems to me, those scriptures speak for themselves. It is your decision whether you want to be the head and not the tail. (I like what *The Living Bible* says here, "...You shall always have the upper hand.")

You may be thinking, *Well, what can I do? I'm already up to my neck in debt.*

If you want to be free just make a commitment before God to get out from under those debts. It won't happen overnight, but it will happen if you'll obey God and stay on the Word.

Remember that $22,000 worth of bad debt I told you about? At the time I committed to God to pay that off and never borrow another dime, it looked to me like I'd never be able to do it. But in faith I sat down and wrote out checks in payment of each debt. Then I put them in a drawer and waited for God to provide the money. As He did, I'd go to the drawer, get out the check and pay off a debt. Within 11 months, I was free and clear of debt. During that time, we began an increase that has never stopped. It is THE BLESSING of God.

"Oh, Brother Copeland, do you think God would enable me to pay off my debts that fast?"

I don't know. How serious are you about the Word? How

much time and attention are you willing to give it? How obedient are you willing to be?

God didn't make it possible for me to pay off my debts just because He liked me a little more than most folks. No, He's no respecter of persons, but He is a respecter of faith. He's a respecter of obedience. So, it's really up to you, isn't it? However you choose to measure it is how He'll measure it back to you.

As you look at your situation right now, you may not be able to see how on earth you could ever get out of debt, much less stay that way. Don't worry, I felt that way too, at first. I just didn't see how I'd ever be able to operate successfully without borrowing money. The bottom line is, you have to trust God!

He knows how and He showed me. He'll do the same for you.

There's no debt too big, no business too complicated for Him to handle. So I think I'm safe in saying He can manage yours. And He can do it without ever borrowing a dime. "And my God will liberally supply (fill to the full) your every need according to His riches in glory in Christ Jesus" (Philippians 4:19, *The Amplified Bible*).

He does it not according to the possibilities of this Earth, but according to His riches *in glory*. Heaven can handle even your situation!

LIVING TO GIVE

Chapter 8
Living to Give

There's one thing you must always remember, however. If you want your needs met according to God's riches in glory, if you want heaven to handle your situation, then you'll have to operate by heaven's principles. You'll have to do things God's way, not man's way—and God always works through the process of sowing and reaping. That process is the basic principle for all of heaven's operations.

Jesus taught us about it in Mark 4:26-32:

So is the kingdom of God, as if a man should cast seed into the ground; And should sleep, and rise night and day, and the seed should spring and grow up, he knoweth not how. For the earth bringeth forth fruit of herself; first the blade, then the ear, after that the full corn in the ear. But when the fruit is brought forth, immediately he putteth in the sickle, because the harvest is come. And he said, Whereunto shall we liken the kingdom of God? or with what comparison shall we compare it? It is like a grain of mustard seed, which, when it is sown in the earth, is less than all the seeds that be in the earth: But when it is sown, it groweth up, and becometh greater than all herbs, and shooteth out great branches; so that the fowls of the air may lodge under the shadow of it.

Seed planting—and harvest. It's the unchangeable law of the kingdom of God and, mysterious as it may seem, it is always working.

We've already seen that your first step in activating this law in the area of finances is to plant the prosperity promises of God into the soil of your heart.

But, it's not enough just to plant the Word.

Not enough!? you ask.

That's right. You can know every prosperity scripture in the Bible. You can walk around confessing them day and night. But you won't reap a financial harvest unless you put some action to your faith, for as James 2:26 says, "...Faith without works is dead also." You have to plant!

In the area of finances, the action that brings your faith to life is that of giving.

Faith in the Word of God—and giving. Those two elements working together will bring forth a harvest of prosperity every time. Notice, I said they must be together. They won't work separately. Faith won't produce without the action of giving. You can give money until you run out, but if you don't couple it with faith in God's Word, you're not guaranteed a return.

Think of the Word as the inner part of the seed. It's the portion that contains the supernatural power to reproduce and bring God's promises to pass. The money, or the gift, is the husk around that seed. It's the tangible substance you can physically plant into a situation so that supernatural power can be released.

Give Your Way to a Miracle

The Bible is filled with accounts of people who, by giving, tapped into the miracle power of God. In 1 Samuel 1, you can read about Hannah, for example. Hannah wanted a child desperately, but she was barren. Year after year, she went to the temple and cried out to God. Year after year, she wept and mourned about it. But nothing happened.

Then one day she went into the temple and said, "O Lord

of hosts, if thou wilt...give unto thine handmaid a man child, then I will give him unto the Lord all the days of his life..." (1 Samuel 1:11).

That gift changed the whole situation. By giving one child to God in faith, God's supernatural power was released in Hannah's life, and she ended up having a whole houseful of children.

She planted a seed and she received a harvest.

"But, Brother Copeland," you say, "I just don't have much to give!"

How much you have doesn't matter. What matters is that you give *something*—and that you give it in faith! There have been times in my life when all I had to put in an offering was the pencil they'd given me to use to write my name on the offering envelope. One time I even pulled a button off my shirt and put it in the plate. (I would have put in the whole shirt if the Lord had asked me!)

Those gifts weren't much, but they were all I had. What's more, they were enough to put the law of giving and receiving in motion.

I believe God is more pleased by a pencil and a button given in faith than He is by a $100 gift given without it. After all, God isn't hurting financially. He already owns everything that exists. What catches His attention is the attitude of the giver.

That's why Jesus responded as He did to the widow who gave her two mites. Let's take a look at that incident as it's recorded in the book of Mark:

Jesus sat over against the treasury, and beheld how the people cast money into the treasury: and many that were rich cast in much. And there came a certain poor widow, and she threw in two mites.... And he called unto him his disciples, and saith unto them, Verily I say unto you,

That this poor widow hath cast more in, than all they which have cast into the treasury: For all they did cast in of their abundance; but she of her want did cast in all that she had, even all her living (Mark 12:41-44).

> To give without expecting to receive a return is spiritually irresponsible.

Just imagine this situation. Jesus was sitting by the treasury as people put in their offerings. Don't you know there was some sanctimonious stuff going on with Him there watching? No doubt, pharisaical robes were swishing grandly as those wealthy leaders strolled by the treasury and put in their gifts that day.

Right in the middle of it all, this poor widow walked up and threw in her offering. I can just see in my mind's eye the determined look on her face. I can hear her saying to herself, *By the eternal, Almighty God who liveth, I've had enough of this poverty. I'm fed up with having nothing but want. I may just be a poor widow now, but I won't be just a poor widow anymore. I'll be completely broke if God doesn't do something here, because I'm giving Him everything I have!*

Then, wham! She threw that last little dab of money into the offering plate.

Did she go completely broke by giving it all? No. A hundred times no! That offering caught Jesus' attention. It connected her to Him and stirred up the anointing of increase in Him and He began to teach. He said, "Listen, everybody. I want to talk to you about this woman..." and He started to preach.

What moved Jesus wasn't just the fact that she gave. It was *how* she gave. She gave in faith—not in fear. She gave of her living. She didn't stop and calculate what she didn't have and say, "Boy, if I do this, tomorrow I won't eat." Instead, she boldly threw in all she had, expecting God to take care of her in return.

Jesus said she had given more than all the rest. It doesn't matter how little you have to give. If you'll start holding your offering up to the Lord in confidence, blessing Him with it, and then releasing it boldly into His service expecting His blessings in return, you'll start seeing some real financial miracles. You'll start reaping harvests that exceed your fondest dreams!

Great Expectations

Right now the theological wheels in your mind are probably starting to turn and you're wondering, *Is he saying I should give expecting to receive?*

Yes, that's exactly what I'm saying. I'll even go one step further and say this: To give without expecting to receive a return is spiritually irresponsible.

You wouldn't think very highly of a farmer who planted his seeds, then let his crop rot in the field while people were starving. If he said, "Well, brother, I don't really want to receive anything in return. I just plant seed for the joy of planting." You wouldn't think he was spiritual, you'd just think he was wrong.

It is just as wrong to give financial seeds and not receive a harvest from them while there are people starving to hear the gospel!

Of course, there are always those who will argue that it is selfish to give expecting something from God in return. But frankly, that baffles me because God teaches us all through the Bible that in His economy giving results in receiving.

Proverbs 19:17, for example, says, "He that hath pity upon the poor lendeth unto the Lord; and that which he hath given will he pay him again."

In Ecclesiastes 11:1, Solomon puts it this way, "Cast thy bread upon the waters: for thou shalt find it after many days."

In Luke 6:38, Jesus said, "Give, and it shall be given unto you; good measure, pressed down, and shaken together, and running over, shall men give into your bosom. For with the same measure that ye mete withal it shall be measured to you again."

Second Corinthians 9:6-11 says:

But this I say, He which soweth sparingly shall reap also sparingly; and he which soweth bountifully shall reap also bountifully. Every man according as he purposeth in his heart, so let him give; not grudgingly, or of necessity: for God loveth a cheerful giver. And God is able to make all grace abound toward you; that ye, always having all sufficiency in all things, may abound to every good work....(Now he that ministereth seed to the sower both minister bread for your food, and multiply your seed sown, and increase the fruits of your righteousness;) Being enriched in every thing to all bountifulness, which causeth through us thanksgiving to God.

In Galatians 6:7-9, the Apostle Paul, encouraging the Galatian Christians to give financially to those who teach them the Word, says:

Be not deceived; God is not mocked: for whatsoever a man soweth, that shall he also reap. For he that soweth to his flesh shall of the flesh reap corruption; but he that soweth to the Spirit shall of the Spirit reap life everlasting. And let us not be weary in well doing: for in due season we shall reap, if we faint not.

Those are just a few examples of the scriptures God has given to teach us the spiritual law of giving and receiving. Did He give us those scriptures so we would pseudopiously ignore that law, acting as if it is ungodly to receive a financial harvest? No, He expected us to put the law of giving and receiving to work in our lives!

God Planted His Seed

If you want to understand just how powerful the law of giving and receiving actually is, consider this: The whole plan of redemption was based on it.

"For God so loved the world, that he gave his only begotten Son, that whosoever believeth in him should not perish, but have everlasting life" (John 3:16). Think about that. God gave one Son so that He could receive many more sons in return.

To those of us who live on this side of the Cross and the Resurrection, it's hard to grasp what a sacrificial gift that really was. But step back in time and view it from God's perspective for a moment.

He had already suffered some tremendous losses. He had lost his top-ranked, most anointed angel, Lucifer, and a third of the angelic hosts. He had lost the man and woman He created because they had bowed their knee to Satan. In addition, because He had given man dominion over the Earth, God had lost access to that Earth through the Fall.

Any way you look at it, that's a lot of real estate down the drain!

What did God use to turn that great loss around? He used the law of giving and receiving.

He knew it would take faith and a sinless sacrifice to turn the situation around. So He gave the best that He had—Jesus.

Can you see the faith God released in sending Jesus?

Mankind had already proven they were capable of rejecting God. They had already done it in the Garden of Eden. What's more, no man had ever taken on death, descended to hell and been resurrected before, as Jesus was about to do.

What guarantee was there that God would ever get Him back? What guarantee was there that mankind would receive the sacrifice He made?

The guarantee was the power of faith in His own Word, released through the law of giving and receiving. God's own Word and its power to bring itself to pass.

God released His faith when He planted His Seed. Therefore, He was assured that although in the man Adam all died, even so in the man Christ Jesus all would be made alive. God knew that when His Seed was planted in faith, it would produce a harvest and no one could stop it. Not the devil and all of hell itself!

Today, God has millions upon millions of sons and daughters, born-again men and women re-created in the image of Jesus. They are the reflection of God's gift. They are the harvest of His Seed planted in faith.

You Can't Get Around It

That's the way the law of seed-plant and harvest works. It is a reflective law. According to that law, what you have now is a reflection of what you have done in the past.

If you put it in financial terms, that law says the material wealth you have received from THE BLESSING of God today is a reflection of what you've previously done with your giving and your faith.

That truth may come as a shock to you. You may say, "Oh, no! I'm poor because of the economy. I'm poor because I was born on the wrong side of town. I'm poor because other people have oppressed me. I didn't have anything to do with it."

Don't try to tell God you didn't have anything to do with it because He has already said He won't be mocked; whatever you sow, you'll reap. The Copeland translation is, "What you put out is what you get back." Not only that, you'll get it back in the same measure you give it.

I don't care how hard you argue, you can't get around it. Do unto others as you would have them do unto you (Matthew 7:12) is not just a golden rule, it's a spiritual law. It's always working—either for you or against you.

You see, a law works like a pendulum. It swings the same distance in one direction as it does in the other. If you're giving in faith, you'll be on the positive side of that swing, enjoying the blessings of an abundant return. If you are withholding because of unbelief, you will be on the negative side of that swing and you'll find yourself losing money every time you turn around.

Proverbs 11:24 says it this way, "There is that scattereth, and yet increaseth; and there is that withholdeth more than is meet, but it tendeth to poverty."

Since that law is always working, there is really no way to steal anything. A thief may think he has stolen something, but he'll end up paying the price no matter how slick an operator he may be. Actually, he'll pay a higher price for it than if he'd gone down and bought that item from the store because "...the way of transgressors is hard" (Proverbs 13:15).

When God was teaching me this principle, He gave me the example of a mechanic who had cheated a customer by charging him for new spark plugs when he'd really just cleaned the old ones and put them back in the customer's car. Now that mechanic thought he'd gotten away with something. He thought he'd made an extra $17 through that sneaky deal.

But the law of seed-plant and harvest was at work. So a few

days later, his air compressor broke down and it cost him $1700 to repair it. Of course, he never connected the two incidents, but the truth was he'd received a hundredfold return on that $17 he'd swindled.

As Solomon would say, that mechanic cast his bread upon the waters and after some days, it returned to him.

Some people would say, "Well, Brother Copeland, I just don't believe that."

It doesn't matter whether they believe it or not, it's still working in their lives. They are standing on the beach and the waves are coming in no matter what they think. If they haven't been casting anything out there, and they've just been sitting around saying, "Nothing good ever happens to me," that's exactly what they'll get—a hundredfold worth of nothing.

> Our *motive* for giving should be our love for the Lord and our desire to bless Him and His people.

But if they've been consistently casting out gifts in faith, eventually they'll have blessings coming in on every wave! I know from experience that's true, because it has happened to me.

I remember when it started years ago. I needed a suit of clothes because I'd given all my clothes away except for one or two suits (and they were too big for me because I'd been losing weight). I had saved and believed God for a new suit because I needed one to wear when I was preaching.

When I finally saved enough money, I went into the store, took the suit off the rack and stepped into the dressing room to try it on. Afterward, I walked up to the counter to pay my bill. I had the cash and I was really feeling prosperous!

But when I handed the clerk the money, he pushed it back across the counter and said, "No, sir. I can't take that. The bill for your suit is already paid. A man came in here and paid for it while you were in the dressing room. He told me not to tell you who he was. He said you're supposed to give God the glory for it."

So I put my money back in my pocket and praised God!

Do you know what I did with that money? I sowed it as seed into other ministries. God provided the suit. He provided the seed. He multiplied the seed sown.

Ever since that time, Gloria and I and our family have lived our lives on that simple principle. It works! It's God's way of life.

A Word About Motives

Some people think those gifts are given to me because I'm a preacher, but that's not so. There are preachers who can't get anyone to give them anything! They can stand in the pulpit and say how much they love chocolate pie and no one will give them one.

That's because they're not givers. They haven't planted seed, so they don't have a harvest coming. They haven't activated the law stated in Ephesians 6 which says we should live "...as the servants of Christ, doing the will of God from the heart; With good will doing service, as to the Lord, and not to men: Knowing that whatsoever good thing any man doeth, the same shall he receive of the Lord, whether he be bond or free" (verses 6-8).

Now most of us will nod when we hear that scripture and say, "Oh, yes, amen. That's right." But the fact is, we don't really believe it. If we believed it, we'd be looking all day for opportunities to do good for other folks, because we'd know that everything we do for others, God will do for us in return. That's the law of His kingdom.

Now, I'm not saying our motive in giving should be to receive. It shouldn't. Our motive should be our love for the Lord and our desire to bless Him and His people.

But let me tell you something important. If you have the love of God in your heart (and according to Romans 5:5, as a believer you do), you may start out giving because you want to receive, but before long, you'll become so swept up in the joy of giving, you'll forget all about your own needs.

You might come home one day and realize you don't have a dime in the bank or a crumb of food in the refrigerator. You'll think, *What have I done? I've become so caught up in this, I've given all my money away and didn't even think to go to the grocery store.*

Then, just about that time somebody will knock on the front door. They'll have a big plate of steaks in one hand and a grill in the other, and they'll say, "We just love you so much, we wanted to come fix you dinner tonight."

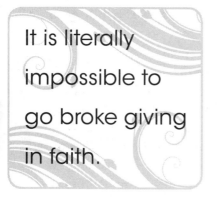

It is literally impossible to go broke giving in faith.

You may think that sounds wild, but it once happened to me. A fellow brought me steaks, a charcoal grill, matches—everything I needed for dinner. Then he gave me the grill before he left!

When you start operating in that kind of giving and receiving, you won't have *more* trouble with wrong motives, you'll have *less!* Material possessions won't stick to you. You'll know it's God who supplied them, and since He is still in the supplying business, it won't bother you to give them away and just keep moving.

You may start out giving to live—but you'll end up living to give.

Your Heavenly Account

"Well now, you have to be careful preaching that living to give message. People will take it and give themselves into the poorhouse."

Not if they give in faith, they won't.

The Bible doesn't say, "Give and you'll go broke, lose everything you have and eventually go under." It says, "Give, and it shall be given unto you; good measure, pressed down, and shaken together, and running over..." (Luke 6:38).

It is literally impossible to go broke giving in faith.

Here's why. Every time you give, it is like making a deposit in a heavenly account. The more you give, the bigger that account grows. Then when you have a need, all you have to do is make a withdrawal by faith.

That's what Jesus was talking about in Matthew 6:19-21, when He said:

Lay not up for yourselves treasures upon earth, where moth and rust doth corrupt, and where thieves break through and steal: But lay up for yourselves treasures in heaven, where neither moth nor rust doth corrupt, and where thieves do not break through nor steal: For where your treasure is, there will your heart be also.

Religious tradition has taught that in this scripture Jesus was referring to the eternal rewards we'll receive when we get to heaven. But He wasn't. If you'll read the surrounding verses you'll see He was explaining how to trust God for things like food and clothing. He was teaching about how to live on Earth.

What Jesus wanted us to understand was that true financial security doesn't come from storing up wealth on the Earth, but from storing it in heaven. The reason is obvious. The world's economy goes up and down. Inflation drains the value of our dollars. Then depression comes and makes those dollars scarce. Thieves, embezzlers and con men will snatch anything and everything they can. Natural disasters like floods, tornadoes and droughts can destroy a fortune overnight.

In my lifetime, I've seen men who were so wealthy in natural terms that it looked as though they'd never run out of money. Yet today, they're completely bankrupt.

As born-again believers and citizens of the kingdom of God, you and I have a spiritual bank in which to store our assets. That bank is totally unaffected by the ups and downs of this world system. It is above the evils of this world and we don't have to wait until we get to heaven to draw on its resources.

Thank God for heaven. It's just one more step on the ladder of blessing and we'll have a great time when we get there. But we need to realize we have access to the benefits of our citizenship there right now. We're already living in the Land of Promise. God has already "...blessed us with all spiritual blessings in heavenly places in Christ" (Ephesians 1:3).

We're still living *in* this world, but we're not *of* it. That's what Jesus said in the prayer He prayed for us right before He went to the cross:

> I have given them thy word; and the world hath hated them, because they are not of the world, even as I am not of the world. I pray not that thou shouldest take them out of the world, but that thou shouldest keep them from the evil. They are not of the world, even as I am not of the world. Sanctify them [in other words, set

them apart from the world] through thy truth: thy word is truth. As thou hast sent me into the world, even so have I also sent them into the world (John 17:14-18).

Astonishing as it may seem, Jesus was actually saying that we are to live like He did when He was on the Earth—not according to the dictates and resources of this world, but according to the dictates and resources of heaven. Think for a moment about how Jesus lived. He didn't worry about rising taxes, He just withdrew resources from His heavenly account when He needed them. He just sent Peter fishing and told him to get the tax money out of the mouth of the first fish he caught.

Jesus didn't worry about the grocery stores running out of food. If He needed more food than the world's system could make available at a certain place and time, He released His faith and used a few loaves and fishes to feed thousands.

God expects us to live the same way. He expects us to be sanctified, or set apart, from this world's economy.

How? By His Word.

If you'll live according to the Word of God, you'll become an answer to the financial problems in this world instead of a victim of them. Inflation, depression and theft won't be able to hurt you. You won't be operating in that realm. You'll be operating above it.

Instead of wringing your hands and worrying about prices going up, you'll be able to cast the care of that over on God and say, "What does it matter if bread costs $30 a loaf? My God is the One who made the wheat that makes the bread—and He'll provide me with the money to buy it regardless of what it costs because He meets my needs according to His riches in glory by Christ Jesus."

You'll stop being so shaken by fluctuations in the world's

system and you'll just stay steady in God. Eventually, you'll start gathering up the riches that are slipping through the fingers of those who have put their trust in the world. I know you will because the Bible says, "...The wealth of the sinner is laid up for the just" (Proverbs 13:22).

Some sinner will sell out in a hurry thinking, *Oh, I'm going to lose everything I have. I'd better sell before it's too late.* But he'll end up selling when the market is on the bottom and buying when it's sky high. Then he'll go around confessing, "I don't understand that. I can't ever seem to get my timing right."

All the while, you'll just keep walking steadily by faith in the Word. You'll just keep prospering. Then when the sinner goes broke, you can go over and bail him out of his jam. You'll become his answer financially and in the end you'll be able to bring him The Answer spiritually.

Once you learn how to lay up treasure in heaven, you won't have to become anxious over the economic evils of this world. You can just take advantage of the situation. When depression hits and banks are selling for pennies on the dollar, you can buy a couple of them. You can hang on to them until the depression is over, then sell them for a hefty profit. When the economy is booming, you can find out where everybody is going, get there first and buy the real estate.

If you don't know where everybody is going, pray in tongues until you find out. Get with the Holy Spirit and find out what's going on instead of just running in this rat race with the rest of the world. Start laying up treasure in heaven. When it's time to make a deal, you'll have the resources to do it!

Start Making Deposits

In the parable of the rich man, Jesus gives us insight into exactly how we lay up treasures in heaven. In Luke 12, He says:

The ground of a certain rich man brought forth plentifully: And he thought within himself, saying, What shall I do, because I have no room where to bestow my fruits? And he said, This will I do: I will pull down my barns, and build greater; and there will I bestow all my fruits and my goods. And I will say to my soul, Soul, thou hast much goods laid up for many years; take thine ease, eat, drink, and be merry.

But God said unto him, Thou fool, this night thy soul shall be required of thee: then whose shall those things be, which thou hast provided? So is he that layeth up treasure for himself, and is not rich toward God. And he said unto his disciples, Therefore I say unto you, Take no thought for your life, what ye shall eat; neither for the body, what ye shall put on. The life is more than meat, and the body is more than raiment.

Consider the ravens: for they neither sow nor reap; which neither have storehouse nor barn; and God feedeth them: how much more are ye better than the fowls? And which of you with taking thought can add to his stature one cubit? If ye then be not able to do that thing which is least, why take ye thought for the rest? Consider the lilies how they grow: they toil not, they spin not; and yet I say unto you, that Solomon in all his glory was not arrayed like one of these.

If then God so clothe the grass, which is today in the field, and tomorrow is cast into the oven; how much more will he clothe you, O ye of little faith? And seek not ye what ye shall eat, or what ye shall drink, neither be ye of doubtful mind. For all these things do the nations of the world seek after: and your Father knoweth that ye have need of these things. But rather seek ye the kingdom of God; and all these things shall be added unto you.

Fear not, little flock; for it is your Father's good pleasure to give you the kingdom. Sell that ye have, and give alms; provide yourselves bags which wax not old, a treasure in the heavens that faileth not, where no thief approacheth, neither moth corrupteth. For where your treasure is, there will your heart be also (verses 16-34).

> Jesus didn't say it's bad to be rich. He said it's bad *not* to be rich toward God.

Look again at those last few lines and you'll see that to lay up treasure in heaven, you must simply do what we've been talking about all along—*give*. Every time you step out in faith and give, you make a deposit in your heavenly account.

Through giving, you are "Laying up in store for themselves [yourself] a good foundation against the time to come..." (1 Timothy 6:19). You are storing up heavenly supplies for the times when the storms of life come your way and the devil tries to steal from you.

Did you know you can't be stolen from if you're a giver?

Someone might take something you didn't intend to give them. But if you'll learn how to give by choice the thing that was stolen, God will get your goods back for you and add a harvest for your giving on top of it!

Then if you'll keep on walking in that realm of giving, you'll eventually become so built up in faith and so surrounded by the angels of God, a thief won't even be able to touch you.

Where Is Your Trust?

Now, before we leave this parable about the rich man, I want you to look again at Luke 12:21. There Jesus says, "So is he that layeth up treasure for himself, and is not rich toward God."

Notice Jesus didn't say it's bad to be rich. He said it's bad *not* to be rich toward God.

It is possible to have an abundance of material possessions and be rich toward God as well. It isn't easy, however. Jesus told His disciples that it's hard "for them that trust in riches to enter into the kingdom of God" (Mark 10:24). Then, to emphasize the point, He added, "It is easier for a camel to go through the eye of a needle, than for a rich man to enter into the kingdom of God" (verse 25).

When His disciples (who were obviously not poor) exclaimed, "Who then can be saved?" Jesus answered, "With men it is impossible, but not with God: for with God all things are possible" (see verses 26-27).

In other words, a rich man can't get into the kingdom of heaven without God. But then, nobody can get into the kingdom of God without God—whether they're rich or poor. So instead of avoiding and condemning material wealth, we need to learn what God has to say about wealth and then deal with it His way.

He gives us the instructions we need in 1 Timothy 6:17-19.

Charge them that are rich in this world, that they be not highminded, nor trust in uncertain riches, but in the living God, who giveth us richly all things to enjoy; That they do good, that they be rich in good works, ready to distribute, willing to communicate; Laying up in store for themselves a good foundation against the time to come, that they may lay hold on eternal life.

Again, please note this scripture doesn't say to charge them that are rich in this world to get rid of everything they have, because God doesn't like people who have things. It doesn't tell us to save one old shiny suit and move off into a cabin in the hills and be humble. If you do that, you simply take yourself out of any position to bless anyone else in the rest of the world. That's the most selfish thing that a Christian could do.

No, these verses simply said the rich shouldn't trust in their riches, but in God. That's an important point. It's something you'll have to deal with where your own mind and flesh are concerned, and the more you prosper, the more you'll have to deal with it.

You'll have to judge yourself every day of your life on your own inner attitude and faith to make sure you're depending on God and not on what you have in the bank. But don't let that scare you. Just make a sober determination that you'll do it.

I know one man who really let this shake him. He came to me and said, "I'm worried. God has already made me worth quite a bit of money and I don't want to get off into an area where I'm not living by faith."

If that's your concern, I'll tell you what I told him.

First of all, don't get upset and worried about it, because

when you do that, you're already abandoning your faith. Faith doesn't worry.

Second, guard against putting your confidence in money by continually tithing and giving of your increase. Obey the instructions Paul gave and be always ready to distribute. That means you'll need to have your ear tuned to God all the time. The moment He says *Give*, you give!

The first time He tells you to give $10 and on the inside you catch yourself thinking twice about it, you'd better give $20. If you still have a cramp in your heart, get your checkbook out and empty it.

I know that sounds strong, but I've done it. I know what I'm talking about. There have been times that afterward I still felt wrong on the inside, but then I'd just say, "Devil, there's no use in your bothering me about this anymore because the money is all gone. It's too late for you to stop me, I've already given every bit of it away."

Well, if I had as much money as some folks, that would be easier for me to do.

If that's what you're thinking, think again. It's not hard to write a check for 75 percent of your assets when you're only worth $25. But when your assets are $150,000, that 75 percent is tougher to let go. That's why you have to be quick and obedient to give right from the beginning.

Don't Be Lazy

If you want to prosper in God, you must always watch yourself in that area. You must be constantly vigilant, constantly building your faith and meditating the Word.

This is work! It's an everyday occupation. You can't be lazy and get it done. Laziness tends to poverty.

I remember one fellow who told me, "I've quit my job and

I'm living by faith. But it's not working like you said it would."
A few days after he told me that, I went by his house to see
him. When I arrived, it was noon, and he was just getting out
of bed.

Listen, God won't pay you for sleeping and neither will
anyone else. He warned us about that when He said, "Yet a
little sleep, a little slumber, a little folding of the hands to sleep;
So shall your poverty come as a robber, and your want as an
armed man" (Proverbs 24:33-34, *The Amplified Bible*).

The person who wants to live by faith must "...labour, working with his hands [or in this natural realm] the thing which is
good, that he may have to give to him that needeth" (Ephesians
4:28). In addition to that, he must work to renew his mind constantly to God's Word and His way of thinking.

When you start living by faith, you don't quit work. You
change employers. You go to work full time for God.

I've seen people believe God for a job and jobs just seem to
jump all over them. Then I've seen other people who believe for
a job and can't find even one.

Personally, if I found myself in that situation, I would be
very careful not to yield to the temptation to say, "See there,
these things don't work for me." They do work. If something is
wrong, it's not with God or faith or His Word. So it must be with
me. The first thing I would do would be to examine myself very
thoroughly. I'd go before God on my knees at the Communion
table. I'd get the cup and the bread in front of me and I'd start
judging myself.

I'd find out if I was holding an offense against somebody
or stepping out of love in some way. That's usually the biggest
problem because it is our commandment that we love one another. Failing to walk in love will stop faith quicker than anything else I know.

The second thing I'd do is make sure I was speaking and acting in faith. You can't just walk around saying, "The Word doesn't work for me," and then spend your days sitting in a chair in your living room waiting for someone to call and give you a good job.

Then again, I suppose you *could* (a number of people do), but if you choose that route, you'd better have a good chair because you'll be sitting there a long time.

If you're believing for a job, act on your faith and get busy. If you can't find anything else to do, get a broom and sweep the church sidewalk—but get to work!

Put the seed-plant and harvest law into operation by giving your labor. I have a friend who did that. When he was a teenager, he wanted to be an airplane mechanic, but nobody would hire him because he was too young. So he went to the airport and told the manager of a certain company that he would work for them for nothing. "I'll do whatever you tell me to do," he said.

The manager took him up on it. "If you're dumb enough to work for nothing, I'm sure we can find something for you to do."

My young friend went to work every morning. He stayed all day long. He'd clean tools, sweep the floor and run errands. But he was always watching, listening and learning.

One day he called his boss. "Can we talk about money now?" he asked.

"No," the boss answered. "I told you when we started this that I wouldn't pay you. I don't have a job for you."

"OK. Since you're not paying me anything, do you think it would be all right if I took at least one day off?"

"I suppose you can do whatever you want to do."

Sure enough, the next day my friend didn't go in to work and before the day was out his boss called him on the phone. "Uh,

> Faith is ready to use money to love people. It never uses people to get money.

we're a little short-handed out here. Could you come on in and give us a hand?"

"Are we going to talk money?" asked my friend.

"Yeah, we'll talk money."

Eventually that young man became one of the major mechanics for American Airlines. And he gained that position at a much earlier age than most.

Can you see what he did? He applied the giving principle. By giving his labor to that company he laid up treasure for himself in heaven, then he drew on that treasure and landed himself a job right here on Earth.

This truth is powerful!

If we'll lay hold of it and activate it faithfully in our lives, we'll grow so prosperous that the world won't be able to hold us. You may think that sounds far-fetched, but it actually happened to Abraham and Lot. They were so blessed, the country they were living in couldn't support them. Their flocks were so huge, they were eating up all the grass!

Imagine what it would be like to have the president come to your door and say, "Friend, you'll have to leave this nation, we can't afford you anymore."

In the case of Abraham and Lot, they had to split up to solve the situation. One of them had to go in one direction where the land was lush and green, and the other one had to go in the opposite direction where the land was dry and barren. Lot chose the good land, so you know what Abraham did?

He applied the principle of seed-plant and harvest. He gave Lot the better land. As a result, Abraham just kept increasing and increasing. He became so rich, in fact, that when Lot and his family were taken captive by the combined armies of four enemy kings, Abraham had enough trained servants to defeat those armies single-handedly.

Then when the king of Sodom offered him some of the spoils of battle, Abraham refused them saying, "I have lift up mine hand unto the Lord, the most high God, the possessor of heaven and earth, That I will not take from a thread even to a shoe-latchet, and that I will not take any thing that is thine, lest thou shouldest say, I have made Abram rich" (Genesis 14:22-23).

That's the kind of attitude God wants. That's the kind of man who doesn't trust in earthly riches but in the living God who gives us richly all things to enjoy!

A Dangerous Responsibility

If you want to prosper like Abraham did, you must develop that attitude of faith and responsibility, not to just be blessed but to be a blessing—always ready to distribute. You *must!* Because money without giving is dangerous. Money actually has no value until it is turned into goods and/or services. For it to have any value on its own, fear has to be applied to it. Fear, then, stops tithing and giving. That's when money for money's sake enters in, or as the scripture calls it, the *love* of money, which is the root of all evil. Faith, on the other hand, is ready to use money to love people. It never uses people to get money.

But we shouldn't shun money because it's dangerous. We must simply be more cautious and more prayerful about it, being watchful to use it properly.

That's not difficult for us. After all, we're a generation that's accustomed to danger. We drive to work every day on freeways that are more dangerous than anything our ancestors ever saw. We live in a world where weapons exist that can blow whole nations apart in a matter of seconds. We know how to handle dangerous things.

God has prepared us to handle dangerous levels of prosperity because it's our responsibility to preach the gospel to all the nations so the end can come and Jesus can return. God already has put the technology to do it into our hands. All we need now is the finances.

Think about that. What would the Apostle Paul have done with $200 million? He couldn't have preached the Word by satellite or on television. He couldn't have bought himself a jet so he could reach more people more quickly. All he could have done was buy himself a boat and a fancier toga.

This is the generation that's been handed the technology to reach the world. The ball is in our court. Some may not want it, but we have it anyway. So it's time we picked it up by faith and got the job done. It's time we started laying up treasure in heaven so we can prosper enough to get the gospel to every person on this planet.

In the next chapter, I'll show you how to lay up treasure in that storehouse through tithing, giving as a praise to God, investing in the gospel, and giving to the poor.

LAYING UP TREASURE—FOUR WAYS TO BLESS AND BE BLESSED

Chapter 9

Laying Up Treasure—Four Ways to Bless and Be Blessed

"All the tithe of the land, whether of the seed of the land, or of the fruit of the tree, is the Lord's: it is holy unto the Lord.... And concerning the tithe of the herd, or of the flock...the tenth shall be holy unto the Lord" (Leviticus 27:30-32).

When it comes to laying up heavenly treasure, tithing is the first subject that must be discussed because it is the cornerstone of real, biblical prosperity. God's financial blessings are reserved for the tither alone.

The person who fails to tithe locks himself out of heaven's supply room. By robbing God, he disqualifies himself from receiving his inheritance of abundance.

I realize those words sound stern, but I'm not the one who originated them. God Himself said them in Malachi 3:8: "Will a man rob God? Yet ye have robbed me. But ye say, Wherein have we robbed thee? In tithes and offerings."

You see, according to the Bible, the first 10 percent of our income does not belong to us. It belongs to God. He owns it. If we use it on ourselves, we've stolen it from Him.

Some people say that's legalistic and refuse to believe it. They think that tithing was under the law, and since we're under grace now, we're not responsible to do it.

Those people are seriously mistaken. No one is living under so much grace that they can rob God and get away with it! What's more, although tithing was a part of the old covenant (that's why Abraham, Isaac and the rest of that group were all so rich), it didn't originate with the law.

We have record of Cain and Abel tithing in Genesis 4. Then again, during the incident I mentioned in the last chapter where

Abraham triumphed over the enemy kings, we find that Abraham also tithed.

> And Melchizedek king of Salem brought forth bread and wine: and he was the priest of the most high God. And he blessed him, and said, Blessed be Abram of the most high God, possessor of heaven and earth: And blessed be the most high God, which hath delivered thine enemies into thy hand. And he [Abram] gave him tithes of all (Genesis 14:18-20).

Abraham tithed 400 years before the law was ever given to Moses. So, obviously tithing was established as a divine ordinance long before the law was given. The law simply served to give it form and procedure.

The New Testament book of Hebrews reveals that tithing also remained after the law was fulfilled. In fact, it shows clearly that tithing is more New Testament than it is Old Testament.

Old Testament tithing was just a shadow of what was to come. Although the old covenant saints were blessed through their tithing, we enjoy even greater blessings through our tithing today, because we bring our tithes to a High Priest who is greater than Melchizedek or any other old covenant priest!

> Just as Melchizedek received Abraham's tithes and blessed him, Jesus, Himself, receives our tithes and blesses us.

When you have time, you should read Hebrews 4-8 and study what God has to say about this subject. But for now, let's just look at a few key scriptures.

[This] hope we have as an anchor of the soul, both sure and stedfast, and which entereth into that within the veil; Whither the forerunner is for us entered, even Jesus, made an high priest for ever after the order of Melchisedec. For this Melchisedec, king of Salem, priest of the most high God, who met Abraham returning from the slaughter of the kings, and blessed him; To whom also Abraham gave a tenth part of all.... And here men that die receive tithes; but there he receiveth them, of whom it is witnessed that he liveth (Hebrews 6:19-20, 7:1-2, 8).

Look at that last sentence again. It says, "Here [meaning here on the Earth] men that die receive tithes; but there [in heaven, within the veil where He has entered] he receiveth them, of whom it is witnessed that he liveth."

Who is *He that liveth?* Jesus, of course!

Just as Melchizedek received Abraham's tithes and blessed him, Jesus, Himself, receives our tithes and blesses us.

Now, consider this. The value of a blessing is proportionate to the resources and authority of the blesser. A poor man with no authority can say, "I bless you" and it doesn't carry much weight, because he doesn't have any power to back it up. If the president of a nation blesses you, however, it's more valuable because he can offer you all the resources and power his nation possesses.

Praise God, we're not just blessed by the president of a nation. When we tithe, we're blessed by Jesus, the Anointed Savior, who says, "All power is given unto me in heaven and in earth" (Matthew 28:18). That's what I call truly *blessed!*

Where Should You Give Your Tithe?

If you'll catch hold of this revelation, it will solve some serious questions for you, questions such as, "To whom should I give my tithe? To the church? To the evangelist who preached the Word that got me saved? To the Bible teacher I listen to every day on television?"

In the light of what the book of Hebrews says, the answer to all those questions is *No!*

Your tithe belongs to Jesus alone. He's the One to whom you tithe, and He is the only One who has any right to tell you where that tithe should go. So you need to spend some time with Him on your knees, and let Him show you by His Spirit and by His Word exactly what He wants you to do with His 10 percent.

If every believer in the Body of Christ would do that, there would be more than enough for every God-ordained ministry. The pastor would have plenty. The evangelist would have plenty. The teacher would have plenty. Everybody would be supplied.

It would put a stop to all the heated debates among ministers about where the tithe belongs. The only reason most of them get upset about the issue is that they don't believe they'll be able to get by without all of it. As one minister said to me, "Well, you know, brother, we're all competing for the same Christian dollar."

That attitude isn't scriptural. We're a body. Our job isn't to compete with one another, it's to help each other. We can see examples in the New Testament of how it's to be done.

The Apostle Paul, for instance, traveled extensively ministering the Word in many different cities. Yet he said the people of the church at Philippi were partners with him in ministry through giving and receiving (Philippians 4:15).

There are churches with that same New Testament attitude today. I remember one time in particular I received a check from such a church. At first I was puzzled as to why the church had sent me a gift, then I found out that the pastor had told the congregation, "If you are bringing your tithe today and there is a specific ministry which has fed you spiritually outside this church, just make note of it and we'll see to it they receive a check."

That pastor truly understood the tithe. He had a revelation of the fact that it belongs to Jesus—not some man, or some organization somewhere. He also had faith in his congregation to hear God's voice and obey His instructions concerning their tithe.

Of course, I realize that kind of purposeful handling of your tithe will take a little time and effort. It's not as easy as just dashing off a quick check and tossing it in the offering plate as it goes by on Sunday morning.

But Jesus is looking for people who are willing to put forth that kind of effort. He is looking for people who will handle their tithing as holy and ask Jesus where He wants His money invested.

Some Common Mistakes

If you're just getting started, let me help you avoid some of the mistakes I often see Christians make in this area of tithing.

For instance, some have come to me and said, "Brother Copeland, I'm using my tithe money to buy preaching tapes. I need to hear them."

That is not a valid use for tithe money. It is not to be spent on yourself, no matter how good the purpose might seem.

God instructs us to "Bring ye all the tithes into the storehouse, that there may be meat in mine [God's] house..." (Malachi 3:10).

That means He intends for you to put your tithe into a place that feeds you spiritually. Usually that will be your local church. (If you're in a church that's not feeding you, find another church!) So, ultimately God will use your tithe to feed you more of His Word, bless you and prosper you spiritually. That's the best deal in the world!

Another mistake people sometimes make is neglecting to separate that first 10 percent from the rest of their income. "After all," they say, "it all belongs to God, and we know we'll end up giving more than 10 percent anyway."

That's wrong. Your money isn't "all God's." He gave 90 percent of it to you. It's yours to enjoy and to use for offerings. The first 10 percent, however, is God's and He expects it to be divided out as such with respect and reverence to Him through the discipline of tithing.

Notice I said the *first* 10 percent. God is to come first—before your bills, before your savings, even before your taxes.

You see, if you don't tithe on your gross income, you're putting the government before God. You're excluding Him from that portion of your income and it won't be blessed. You'll find yourself always struggling to scratch up the tax money you need because God isn't involved in it.

That doesn't make good sense to me. I need all the help with my taxes I can get, so here's what I do. I tithe on the gross, then I take my tithe and my tax money both to God and ask Him to bless them.

I use that opportunity to pray for the government. I might say something like, "Lord, the United States government allows me to deduct the money that I give into Your work. That makes them partners with me in my giving. So I bring my tithe and my tax money both before You and ask You to bless them, and to bless the president and this nation."

Ever since the day I began that practice, I've had enough money to pay my taxes on time even when it took supernatural power to get that money to me. I've also stopped grumbling and fussing about it. I pay my taxes with thanksgiving to God and in obedience to the instructions God gives in Romans 13.

Let every soul be subject unto the higher powers. For there is no power but of God: the powers that be are ordained of God. Whosoever therefore resisteth the power, resisteth the ordinance of God: and they that resist shall receive to themselves damnation.

For rulers are not a terror to good works, but to the evil. Wilt thou then not be afraid of the power? do that which is good, and thou shalt have praise of the same: For he is the minister of God to thee for good.

But if thou do that which is evil, be afraid; for he beareth not the sword in vain: for he is the minister of God, a revenger to execute wrath upon him that doeth evil.

Wherefore ye must needs be subject, not only for wrath, but also for conscience sake. For this cause pay ye tribute also: for they are God's ministers, attending continually upon this very thing. Render therefore to all their dues: tribute to whom tribute is due; custom to whom custom; fear to whom fear; honour to whom honour (verses 1-7).

As you can see from those verses, there is no scriptural excuse for violating the tax laws of the land. A Christian has no business giving away a bag of worn-out clothes and then charging them off

> As believers, we must conduct ourselves justly and righteously.

their taxes as if they were new. That's not right and God won't bless it.

Jesus rebuked the Pharisees for such behavior, saying:

Woe to you, scribes and Pharisees, pretenders—hypocrites! for you give a tenth of your mint and dill and cummin, and have neglected and omitted the weightier (more important) matters of the Law, right and justice and mercy and fidelity. These you ought...to have done, without neglecting the others (Matthew 23:23, *The Amplified Bible*).

As believers we must lay aside every kind of lying, cheating and stealing (even from the government) and conduct ourselves justly and righteously. We should be honest and straightforward even if in the short run it looks like it will cost us money.

Christians ought to be that way about everything. We ought to be honest with ourselves, honest with our government, and honest as a witness before the world. That is basic Christian conduct and it's mandatory for anyone who wants to enjoy the prosperity of God.

A Two-Part Command

With all that said, let's go to the book of Deuteronomy and take another look at this process of tithing. There in the 26th chapter, God gives the Israelites specific instructions about how they are to bring their tithes once they reach the Promised Land.

And it shall be, when thou art come in unto the land which the Lord thy God giveth thee for an inheritance, and possessest it, and dwellest therein; That thou shalt take of the first of all the fruit of the earth, which thou shalt bring of thy land that the Lord thy God giveth thee, and shalt put it in a basket, and shalt go unto the place which the Lord thy God shall choose to place his name there. And thou shalt go unto the priest that shall be in those days, and say unto him, I profess this day unto the Lord thy God, that I am come unto the country which the Lord sware unto our fathers for to give us (verses 1-3).

(As you read this, realize that as believers, you and I have entered into our promised land. We have already inherited the promises of God. So, just like the Israelites, we're to take the tenth of our increase and bring it to Jesus. Since God has put His name directly on us as members of the Body of Christ, we don't have to go to a particular building. We can go directly to the Lord, Himself, our High Priest.)

And the priest shall take the basket out of thine hand, and set it down before the altar of the Lord thy God. And thou shalt speak and say before the Lord thy God, A Syrian ready to perish was my father, and he went down into Egypt, and sojourned there with a few, and became there a nation, great, mighty, and populous: And the Egyptians evil entreated us, and afflicted us, and laid upon us hard bondage: And when we cried unto the Lord God of our fathers, the Lord heard our voice, and looked on our affliction, and our labour, and our oppression: And the Lord brought us forth out of Egypt with a mighty hand, and with an outstretched arm, and with great terribleness, and with signs, and with wonders: And he hath brought us into this place, and hath given us this land, even a land that floweth with milk and honey. And now, behold, I have brought the firstfruits of the land, which thou, O Lord, hast given me. And thou shalt set it before the Lord thy God, and worship before the Lord thy God (verses 4-10).

Now, you might be tempted to stop there and think that all there is to tithing is to bring your tenth to Jesus, thank Him for bringing you out of the bondage and captivity of the devil, and then worship God. Without a doubt, that would be a good start, but tithing doesn't end there.

> God also says that once you've received those blessings, the devil won't have any right to steal them from you.

There's more to it! Read on and you'll see what I mean. "Then thou shalt say before the Lord thy God.... Look down from thy holy habitation, from heaven, and bless thy people Israel, and the land which thou hast given us..." (verses 13, 15).

Can you see what God is showing us there? He's revealing to us that tithing is a two-part command. The first part is to give to Him the tenth in gratitude and worship—and the second part is to receive from Him THE BLESSING that belongs to the tither.

We're *commanded* to receive the return on our tithe! God commanded us to say, "Bless me!"

Yet countless Christians have refused to say anything to God about blessing them because they don't want Him to think they're "trying to buy" their blessings.

If that fear has kept you from expecting a return on your tithe, get rid of it. You're not trying to buy God's blessings; you're just being obedient to Him. You're accepting your full responsibility as a tither, which is to receive as well as to give.

What is this blessing you're receiving? It's described in Malachi 3:10-12:

> Bring ye all the tithes into the storehouse, that there may be meat in mine house, and prove me now herewith, saith the Lord of hosts, if I will not open you the windows of heaven, and pour you out a blessing, that there shall not be room enough to receive it. And I will rebuke the devourer for your sakes, and he shall not destroy the fruits of your ground; neither shall your vine cast her fruit before the time in the field, saith the Lord of hosts. And all nations shall call you blessed: for ye shall be a delightsome land, saith the Lord of hosts.

God says if you're a tither, He'll open the windows of heaven and pour you out a blessing. That's astounding when you think about it. The Bible says God opened the windows of heaven to release the flood of water that destroyed the Earth in Noah's day. Now He's talking about opening those windows to release that same volume of blessing to you!

He also says that once you've received those blessings, the devil won't have any right to steal them from you. That doesn't mean he won't try. It simply means that when the devil comes, you can point your finger at him and tell him to take his filthy hands off your stuff. You can remind him that Almighty God has rebuked him for your sake and his power over you financially has been stopped.

Then, as we say in West Texas, you can tell him to *git!* And like it or not, he'll have to leave your house.

An Economy of Abundance

The blessings of the tither are actually so tremendous that some people have trouble believing them. They say, "Well, I just don't know how God could get that kind of prosperity to me. After all, the economy isn't very good right now."

Listen, heaven's economy is doing fine, and it's heaven's economy you're tapping in to when you tithe.

"But I'm living in this world!"

Yes, but you're not under its dominion. The Bible says in Colossians 1 that God has "delivered us from the power of darkness, and hath translated us into the kingdom of his dear Son" (verse 13). To be translated means to be taken out of one place and put over into another. In other words, your citizenship is not primarily of this Earth. You are not primarily American or Canadian or Australian, you are first and foremost a citizen of the kingdom of God.

That means this planet doesn't have any right to dictate to you whether your needs are met or not. The Bible says God will meet your needs according to His riches in glory! (Philippians 4:19). The problem is, most believers limit God's blessings by expecting Him to meet their needs according to the meager supplies of this world.

They remind me of a friend of mine who was born and raised in the U.S.S.R. about the time of World War II. For years all he and his family knew were persecution and scarcity. They lived on the run, first from the Germans, then from the communists. They ate out of trash cans until they were finally caught and sent to a prison camp.

Eventually, through some miracles of God and the prayers of a couple of grandmothers, they were able to get away and come to the United States. The first place they went when they arrived in this country was a grocery store.

Can you imagine what it was like coming out of a concentration camp and going into an American grocery store? They just walked up and down the aisles of that store and wept for joy at the abundance that was available.

If you would only wake up to the abundance of heaven that's been made available to you, that's how you'd feel too. You'd realize you've been translated out of a world of poverty and into a kingdom that flows with milk and honey.

God meant for us to come to that realization every time we tithe. He meant for us to give our tithe as a way of activating heaven's economy in our lives. So when you bring your tithe to the Lord, make it a time of rejoicing. Make it a time of realizing anew that you've been translated from a world of scarcity to a heavenly economy of abundance.

Here's a prayer to help you get started.

Father, I thank You and praise You for translating me from the kingdom of darkness into the kingdom that You have prepared for me. Thank You that it is a kingdom of mercy, joy and abundance.

I bring my tithe now to You, Lord Jesus. It is the first fruits of what You have given me, and I plant it in Your kingdom as a seed of blessing, expecting the rich blessings of heaven to be multiplied to me in return.

I thank You, Lord, that You've rebuked Satan for my sake, and I stand in agreement with Your Word that he'll not destroy my land. He'll not destroy my blessings, and he'll not destroy my crop in the field. I am a citizen of Your kingdom. I have the rights and privileges of that kingdom and I stand upon them. Thank You, Jesus, that heaven's unlimited resources are mine in Your Name. Amen!

Giving to the Poor

Why would you want to feed the whole county? First, because the love of God in your heart compels you to be a blessing to people, and second, because giving to the poor is yet another way to lay up treasure in heaven.

During Jesus' earthly ministry, He revealed that truth to a rich Jewish ruler. If that ruler had understood and acted upon Jesus' instructions, he could have become richer still. But, like far too many Christians today, he thought Jesus was trying to take something away from him rather than add something to him so he missed out on the opportunity of a lifetime.

Let's take a look at the story and see exactly what happened.

And when he [Jesus] was gone forth into the way, there came one running, and kneeled to him, and asked him, Good Master, what shall I do that I may inherit eternal life? And Jesus said unto him, Why callest thou me good? there is none good but one, that is, God. Thou knowest the commandments, Do not commit adultery, Do not kill, Do not steal, Do not bear false witness, Defraud not, Honour thy father and mother. And he answered and said unto him, Master, all these have I observed from my youth. Then Jesus beholding him loved him, and said unto him, One thing thou lackest: go thy way, sell whatsoever thou hast, and give to the poor, and thou shalt have treasure in heaven: and come, take up the cross, and follow me. And he was sad at that saying, and went away grieved: for he had great possessions (Mark 10:17-22).

It's important to remember when you're reading about this incident, that this young man was extremely well-versed in the Old Testament scriptures. He knew the Abrahamic covenant. He had meditated on the laws and promises contained in it.

It was no accident that this man was rich. Just as God instructed in Joshua 1:8, he had meditated in the law day and night and, as a result, he became prosperous and successful. He was a walking demonstration of God's faithfulness to the promise He gave in Deuteronomy 28:1, 11:

> And it shall come to pass, if thou shalt hearken diligently unto the voice of the Lord thy God, to observe and to do all his commandments...that the Lord thy God will set thee on high above all nations of the earth.... And the Lord shall make thee plenteous in goods, in the fruit of thy body, and in the fruit of thy cattle, and in the fruit of thy ground....

Now, if Jesus had spoken to a gentile, who was ignorant of the Word of God, and asked him to sell all he had and give to the poor, it would be easy to see why he might have thought Jesus was trying to make him poor. But this young man knew the scriptures. When he heard Jesus say, "Give to the poor," he should have immediately thought of Proverbs 19:17, "He that hath pity upon the poor lendeth unto the Lord; and that which he hath given will he pay him again."

He should have remembered Isaiah 48:17, "Thus saith the Lord, thy Redeemer, the Holy One of Israel; I am the Lord thy God which teacheth thee to profit, which leadeth thee by the way that thou shouldest go."

He had already acknowledged Jesus as a prophet of God. So he should have jumped up and said, "Glory to God, this

Prophet is showing me the way to profit! I'm already prosperous, but He is showing me how to be more prosperous still! He is leading me in the way I should go."

That was, in fact, what Jesus was doing. He realized there was something wrong in that man's life. He didn't have any joy or life about him. So Jesus told him how to fix that lack.

Jesus didn't tell him to sell everything, give to the poor and go broke. He said, "Sell what you have, give to the poor and make a connection with heaven." That's the one thing this young man had never done. He had never been a giver.

If he had believed God's promise to repay him for everything he gave, he wouldn't have been grieved, he would have been thrilled. If he had caught sight of the fact that the Master had offered to get into business with him, he would have thought, *What a marvelous opportunity! I have great possessions. There's no telling what Jesus and I together can do to eliminate poverty.*

If he had taken that attitude and started selling, he wouldn't have been able to sell fast enough. His wealth would have increased more quickly than he could have given. He would have made more money than he'd ever made in his life thus far, but his motives would have changed. He would have had Jesus on his heart.

If he had any troubles, he could have gone to Him and said, "Master, You're the One who told me to do this. Tell me how to get the best price for that grain elevator over there. I want to sell it because I've found a whole village of poor folks, and I want to do something to help them."

He would have had a great time!

I personally believe Jesus planned for that young man to become Judas' replacement. After all, he was a wealthy man. He knew how to deal with money. Wouldn't he have made a good treasurer?

What's more, the only men who were asked to leave all and follow Jesus were those who ended up being apostles. This young man could have stepped into position after Judas killed himself, and the disciples wouldn't have had to draw lots for his replacement (see Acts 1:26).

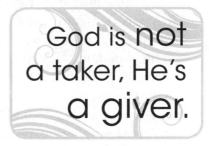

God is not a taker, He's a giver.

But none of that happened, because when it came right down to it, the rich young ruler didn't believe the Word. He was simply religious about it. He knew it with his mind but he didn't believe it with his heart. As a result, the spirit of grief came in and broke his connection with Jesus.

We need to learn from that young man's experience that when God says give to the poor, He is planning more prosperity for us, not less. God is not a taker, He is a giver. So even though what He says sometimes sounds to natural ears like He's trying to take away from us, He's not. He is trying to increase our wealth a hundredfold.

That's what He was trying to do for the rich young ruler. We know that because right after he walked away grieved, Jesus turned to His disciples and said,

Verily I say unto you, There is no man that hath left house, or brethren, or sisters, or father, or mother, or wife, or children, or lands, for my sake, and the gospel's, But he shall receive an hundredfold now in this time, houses, and brethren, and sisters, and mothers, and children, and lands, with persecutions; and in the world to come eternal life (Mark 10:29-30).

You remember that the next time you have an opportunity to buy groceries for someone or help your church's outreach to the poor. Don't see it as loss, see it as an investment that will not only bless people, but will also bring you a rich return.

How rich will that return be? Proverbs 28:8 puts it this way, "He that by usury and unjust gain increaseth his substance, he shall gather it for him that will pity the poor."

Considering the interest rates I've seen in my lifetime, I'd say half the financial institutions in the world have increased their substance by usury and unjust gain. So according to the Bible, that money belongs to the Body of Christ.

Until now, we haven't received much of it because we haven't had much pity on the poor. When we did, we've robbed God of the return He wanted to give us by failing to expect Him to bless us (with a hundredfold measure) as He promised.

I challenge you to change that in your own life today. Begin to give generously to the poor, faithfully trusting God to keep His Word. Give God the opportunity to pour into your hands the treasures wicked men have heaped together for the last days (James 5:3). Let Him begin to bless you with the abundant prosperity you need to help finance the preaching of the gospel to the world.

Giving as a Praise to God

The last method of laying up treasure for yourself in heaven that I want to mention is giving as a praise to God.

When you give as a praise to God, you aren't necessarily giving to meet a specific need. In fact, your focus is not on earthly things at all. It's completely on God. In this type of giving, you take of what you have (meager as it may seem to be), then offer it to Him in gratitude for His goodness and in confidence that

He will be true to His Word and multiply it back to you again.

You may not have any money to give, but that doesn't matter. God will receive whatever you bring, as long as it's brought in love and in faith. In fact, if you'll read Exodus 25, you'll find that when God asked the Israelites for such an offering, He didn't tell them to bring money, He asked them to bring *things*.

And the Lord spake unto Moses, saying, Speak unto the children of Israel, that they bring me an offering: of every man that giveth it willingly with his heart ye shall take my offering. And this is the offering which ye shall take of them; gold, and silver, and brass, and blue, and purple, and scarlet, and fine linen, and goats' hair, and rams' skins dyed red, and badgers' skins, and shittim wood (verses 1-5).

God was specifically planning to use these things in the building of His temple. But then, as now, what delighted Him most was that His people willingly gave to Him of their very best possessions.

There is something very personal and deeply spiritual about such giving. I had a firsthand, close-up realization of that years ago when I saw it in action among the Navajo Indian people.

I had gone to northern Arizona to preach for Kenneth Begishe, a young faith-filled Navajo pastor who had recently started a little church on the Navajo Indian reservation. Now when I say he started a church, I don't mean he rented a nice brick building and printed ads in the newspaper letting people know what time services would be held. I mean he took a little trailer, parked it out in the middle of the reservation where there wasn't anything except brush and red sand. Then he went out and started witnessing to the Navajo sheepherders one on one. He went from hogan to hogan telling the story of Jesus and ministering to people—hurting people, sick people, people who needed a shepherd. He won most of them one by one to Jesus. Then he started a church called White Post Church.

At the time I was there, he had a congregation of about 200 people who had been born again and filled with the Holy Spirit. When I came to preach for him, I told him I wouldn't receive any offerings from him. The Lord had instructed me to consider it a mission venture and so I said, "I respect your desire to bless me but I'm here to give, not to receive."

Now this is beside the point but, pastors, while I'm on this subject I'd like to say that if people come to you asking to work for your church for nothing, then it's fine to receive their services as a gift. But don't try to build a church staff out of free workers. That is contrary to the Word of God.

God never asked anyone to do anything for nothing. He said the laborer is worthy of his hire. He pays people more than they're worth—not less. So if you're having trouble paying your workers, don't try to get them to serve you for free. Get together with them and agree in prayer that God will send money enough to fund the church and everyone who is working in it.

Now, Brother Begishe had an understanding of God's promises of prosperity so he said to me, "OK, Brother Copeland. I'll let you give into our church in that way, but unless you object, I will still continue to receive offerings in these meetings. You see, I have taught my people to give as a praise to God. When I first started this church, not one of my congregation had a vehicle to drive. Many walked, a few had horses and a few drove (horse-drawn) wagons. But today every family is either driving a car or a pickup truck. They've prospered by giving in faith and I want them to keep it up."

Each night during those meetings, the pastor put the

offering bucket on the platform. He taught briefly on the Word of God and sowing and reaping. Then he invited the people to bring their offerings. I had the privilege of watching as these people brought the best they had to give. In some cases, that best was simply a rock they'd polished until it looked nice. In other cases, the offering might be a highly prized garment. But in every case it was something special to the person bringing the gift to God.

Do you know what happened as a result of that kind of giving? Those people kept on prospering. Their incomes grew and they were able to support the church and even build a new building. They were some of the first Navajo believers to grow beyond dependence on an outside missionary organization to having their own churches led by Navajo pastors. White Post Church became the mother church to more than 25 churches in the western part of the 23,000-acre reservation that is home to 230,000 Native Americans. Eventually the church was able to begin reaching out to the distant areas of Arizona and New Mexico's back country and preaching to thousands of tribal people who didn't speak English and who had never heard the Name of Jesus.

One of the most effective forms of giving as a praise to God, as seen in the lives of these faith-filled Navajo believers, is to give when it seems you can least afford to do so. It is a way to praise God by faith in advance for what He has promised to do for you.

I remember one time in particular when I gave in that way. It was years ago when I was first starting out in the ministry. I had traveled several hundred miles to preach a meeting and had spent all I had just getting there. What's worse, the first night's offering was only $4.25 and the pastor of the church had already told me that even if I stayed a month, he couldn't guarantee me $50.

So there I was, a stack of bills due, more coming due, and my wife's birthday coming up in a couple of weeks. Day after day passed, meeting after meeting. The offerings remained so low that the pastor wouldn't even count them. He just poured them into a paper sack and stuffed it into my pocket.

Finally one day the Lord said, *What do you have in your pocket, Kenneth?*

"Thirty-three dollars," I answered. That was the offering total up to that time.

I knew even then what He was about to do. He was about to ask me to give that money to Him. But I didn't want to let go of it. Even though I realized it wasn't enough to pay my bills, it was enough to barely make my way back home.

Of course, God didn't want me to let go of that money because He didn't want me to have it. He wanted me to put it into His hands as seed so He could multiply it according to His riches in glory and give it back to me.

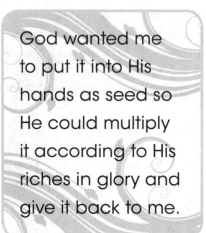

God wanted me to put it into His hands as seed so He could multiply it according to His riches in glory and give it back to me.

Kenneth, how much money were you believing Me for when this meeting began? He asked. *What were you confessing you'd receive?*

When I told Him, He pointed out that the $33 was approximately 10 percent, or the tithe, on that amount. *Why don't you give that money as a praise unto Me?*

Suddenly, I caught the vision. "I'll do it!" I told Him. "I am standing on Your Word that You meet all my needs according to

Your riches in glory by Christ Jesus. And I am so confident that Word is true, I'll tithe in advance on the amount I need, praising You and thanking You for Your faithfulness to me!"

That very day, I took the pastor of the church to town and bought him a new pair of shoes. Back then you could buy a fairly nice pair of shoes for less than $30. Then I put the rest of it in his hand as a blessing.

As the meetings continued, I just kept on believing God and the pastor just kept on putting the offerings in that paper sack. After two weeks, we concluded the meetings. I took the paper money out of the sack and left the change in it. When I counted out the bills I realized I'd ended up having the best two weeks financially that I'd ever had up to that time.

I came home with $1,000 in paper money and a sack full of change. I didn't even know how much was in that sack, I just took it home and gave it to Gloria for her birthday.

Before I could even unpack my clothes, she said, "Let's go shopping. There's a pair of shoes and a purse I want to buy." We went straight to the store. She took those shoes and that purse up to the counter and handed that sack of change to the salesclerk to pay for it.

The clerk could hardly believe what she was seeing. She opened the sack and poured out all those quarters, dimes, pennies and nickels—and started counting. Sure enough, the amount of money in that sack was enough to pay the bill.

"Well, one thing is for sure," laughed the clerk, "I broke you!"

"No you didn't!" said Gloria. "There is more where that came from!"

We were so excited that day about the faithfulness of God, we could hardly stand it. We've never quite gotten over that excitement either. In fact, He has been so faithful to us over the years that I not only enjoy giving what He tells me to give, I like to give more!

There have been times when God would speak to me and say, *I want you to give that man $10.*

I'd say, "All right, Lord. I'll give him $10. But I have $15 in my pocket and if You'll allow me to, I'd like to give him that extra five as a praise to You."

How do you think God responds to that? With great delight, that's how!

As a parent, wouldn't you be delighted if you told your child to go mow the yard and he responded by saying, "Mom and Dad, I love you so much, I'll not only mow it, I'll trim it too!" You can just imagine the effect that would have on you.

Most children don't say things like that because they're too immature to truly value their parents. That's how I was when I was younger. When my dad asked me to help him in the yard, I fought it as much as I could and I certainly never offered to do anything extra.

But when I grew up and learned how precious my parents were, when I realized how much they had given to me, I began to search for opportunities to bless them. That's the way grown Christians ought to be about their heavenly Father. When He says, *I want you to invest some money in that ministry there,* or *I want you to give to those poor people because they don't have enough to eat,* we should be thrilled to do it.

We ought to say, "Father, I love You so much and I praise You so much for helping me to have enough to give, I'm going to skip supper tonight so I'll have a little extra to add to my giving. That way I can give not only what You've asked, but even more!"

When you respond to God in that way, get ready because He will bless you coming in and going out. You'll tap in to an abundance you never dreamed was available when you start giving as a praise to the Lord.

Tapping In to the Hundredfold Return

Once you've laid the foundation of tithing, you'll be ready to lay up treasures in your heavenly account by giving offerings.

An offering is a gift you give to God that is over and above your tithe. It's literally impossible to give offerings without tithing, because until you've given God the 10 percent that belongs to Him, every amount you give is simply what you owe Him.

Once the tithe is tithed, however, you're ready to swim out into even deeper waters of God's blessing. You're ready to receive God's hundredfold return.

Hundredfold return? you ask.

Yes! Jesus promised us a hundredfold return on everything we invest in the kingdom of God. I know that sounds too good to be true. In fact, I wouldn't believe it myself if Jesus, Himself, hadn't said it. But He did! You can read it for yourself in Mark 10:29-30. There, Jesus told His disciples:

> Verily I say unto you, There is no man that hath left house, or brethren, or sisters, or father, or mother, or wife, or children, or lands, for my sake, and the gospel's, But he shall receive an hundredfold now in this time, houses, and brethren, and sisters, and mothers, and children, and lands, with persecutions; and in the world to come eternal life.

Some people refuse to believe that scripture because they say they've never received a hundredfold return on the offerings they've given. I'm sure they haven't. But it's not because Jesus hasn't made it available to them. It's because they haven't exercised their faith to receive that kind of return.

Remember, every promise of God is received by faith. The more your faith grows, the more you can appropriate what belongs to you in Christ Jesus. I'm receiving a greater return on my giving now than I did when I first started back in the 1960s. That's because I've spent time in the Word, reading and studying it. I've built my faith, and I intend to keep on building it and increasing my capacity to receive the full measure of that hundredfold promise.

"But Brother Copeland," you may say, "I'm just now learning about prosperity. I don't have much faith built up at all."

Don't let that discourage you. Just think, even if you had only a third of the faith you needed to receive the hundredfold return Jesus promised, you'd still be able to receive a thirtyfold return. That means every time you gave, your heavenly account would be credited with 30 times the amount of your gift. *Thirty times!* There's no bank in the world that can offer such an extraordinary investment opportunity.

Once you understand that, you won't be wondering anymore whether or not to give offerings. You'll just want to know where to put them!

Investing in the Gospel

One of the first and most obvious places to plant an offering is into the gospel itself by investing in the lives and ministries of those who preach the Word. The Apostle Paul gives us clear instruction about that in Galatians 6:6-7:

"Let him that is taught in the word communicate unto him that teacheth [or as *The Amplified Bible* says, contribute to his support] in all good things. Be not deceived; God is not mocked: for whatsoever a man soweth, that shall he also reap."

Notice that scripture didn't say to give to the preachers who cry the loudest and seem to be in the most desperate need. It simply says, Give to those who teach you the Word.

We're to give because God says to give, and we're to give as He directs—not because we've been emotionally pressured into it.

Personally, I've resolved never to spend my ministry air time or my time in the pulpit pleading for money. If this ministry has a crisis, I'll never write you a letter about it. I'll just take my need to God and trust Him to tell you if He wants you to do something to help.

That doesn't mean, however, that I criticize those in the ministry who do ask for money. In part, I understand it. They're concerned that if they don't keep talking about their needs, Christians won't give.

All too often, they're right.

Countless Christians sit around waiting to "feel led" to give to the ministry. If someone gives a tearful, high-pressure plea for money, the "feeling" comes. If not, it doesn't.

But the truth is, God has already commanded us to give in His written Word. He doesn't say anything about waiting around for some emotional urge. He says we should purpose in our hearts to give (see 2 Corinthians 9:7). Certainly we must be open to hear God's voice and be led by His Spirit about *where* we should invest our offerings, but we'd be much more apt to hear His voice if we had already determined to be obedient to the Bible and base our giving on His Word instead of our feelings.

Now don't misunderstand. I'm not saying that if you don't give, God's ministers will be left financially stranded. God will always find a way to supply the needs of a minister who is standing in faith. He'll be faithful to keep His promise even if He has to pull that provision out of a fish's mouth or fly it in by ravens.

But that's not how God prefers to prosper His ministers. He prefers to do it through your giving because that way He can bless you in the process.

The best way I know to get rich is to start giving to a minister who has been called by God to do more than he can possibly afford. If you'll do that, God will see to it that you prosper so he can prosper. He'll bless you with more so you can give more and have an abundance left over besides!

That's what happened to the boy who gave Jesus his lunch (see John 6:1-13). Jesus took that little lunch, blessed it, multiplied it and used it to feed a multitude. When He was finished there were 12 baskets of food left.

To whom do you think those leftovers belonged? The little boy, of course!

Can't you just imagine that boy coming home dragging all those baskets behind him? I can almost hear his mother saying, "Where did you get all that food, son?"

"Down at that Holy Ghost preacher's meeting, Mama! I gave Him my lunch. He fed it to a few thousand people and then gave me the leftovers!"

"Well, let's go back again tomorrow, boy. Maybe the preacher will let you feed that crowd again!"

That's the way God planned to finance His ministers— through people so excited about giving, you can't stop them from it. He doesn't want to have to pry your offerings out of unwilling hands. But because of the disobedience of God's people, ministers have had to do it ever since the Israelites crossed into the Promised Land.

At that time, God had given Moses specific instructions about providing for the priests (or Levites). Since they were to serve as ministers to the Lord, they were to be funded by the people of Israel instead of having to work the land for themselves. God had clearly said, "Command the children of Israel, that they give unto the Levites of the inheritance of their possession cities to dwell in; and ye shall give also unto the Levites suburbs for the cities round about them" (Numbers 35:2). "Take heed not to forsake or neglect the Levite [God's minister] as long as you live in your land" (Deuteronomy 12:19, *The Amplified Bible*).

Despite those instructions from God, however, when the Israelites arrived in the Promised Land, they divided everything up among the other eleven tribes—and nobody said a word to the Levites.

> Then the heads of the fathers' houses of the Levites came to Eleazar the priest and Joshua son of Nun, and the heads of the fathers' houses of the Israelite tribes; They said to them...The Lord commanded by Moses that we should be given cities to dwell in..." (Joshua 21:1-2, *The Amplified Bible*).

I can just hear those Levites, "Excuse me, sirs—EXCUSE ME! God told you to provide for us and you haven't done it!" That was the first *appeal letter* and it seems like preachers have been writing them ever since. Month after month, ministers have had to say, "Hey, God told me to go preach in Africa. I need you to give! God told me to build a building. I need you to give! God has instructed me to evangelize the inner cities. Help me!"

If they don't call for help one month, many believers will let them go down the drain financially without giving it a thought. That's a disgrace, and for the Body of Christ to enjoy the prosperity God has promised, that situation will have to change.

It's already changing to a great extent. I've seen it in this ministry. Gloria and I have Partners who are so determined to help us do what God has commanded us to do that we don't ever write letters asking them for money. They're Partners!

They give because they are in this ministry with us.

They don't forget us. They pray for us every day. They send us letters of encouragement and gifts, not because we asked them for it, but because they love Jesus with all their hearts and they want to give into His work. They are committed!

My, those people are precious to us. Even more importantly, they're precious to God, and He will pour all the blessings on them they can stand, because He is so delighted with them. Over the years, many of them have become rich and many more of them are on their way because He knows He can trust them.

> God never asks you for more than He can give you.

What's Your Assignment?

If you're determined to be that kind of giver, here's a word of wisdom to help you be more effective. Don't just scatter your offerings in every direction. Don't sling them at random like grass seed, letting them fall where they may.

Go to God and ask Him to reveal to you where He wants you to focus your giving. Ask Him to reveal to you what ministries you've been especially called and assigned to support, so you can give with greater purpose and power.

I remember one of the first times God gave me a giving assignment. He spoke to me and told me to give $50,000 into Kenneth Hagin Ministries. That was many years ago when I didn't have $50 to my name—much less $50,000!

"How will I do that, Lord?" I asked.

Don't wait until you have the whole $50,000. Start by giving what you have, He answered. *Then as your harvest comes, give more.*

So I obeyed. I gave the few dollars that I had, then I went to work on that assignment. I sent a portion of every dollar that came through my hands to Kenneth Hagin Ministries. Before long I was completely caught up in it. I had tunnel vision. I was consumed by the vision of giving $50,000 into that ministry.

I constantly confessed, "Thank God, in the Name of Jesus, I am prosperous. I have the money I need to invest in Brother Hagin's ministry. The Lord makes my way prosperous. He takes pleasure in the prosperity of His servant and I'm His servant."

I started enjoying myself so much I almost forgot about the $50,000 goal. I just gave everything I could. I even sent Bibles to Brother Hagin (as if Kenneth Hagin didn't have enough Bibles!).

Then one day the Lord prompted me to call and ask them to total up my giving, so I could see how I was doing on my assignment. Much to my surprise, I found out I had gone beyond the $50,000 mark. I had no idea where I'd gotten all that money. But I did know that I had prospered like never before because I had focused in on what God had instructed me to do.

Of course, when you receive an assignment like that, don't completely stop scattering grass seeds. Keep giving here and there. Bless people wherever you can, but keep the main thrust of your giving trained on your assignment. Let that assignment take hold of your heart until you're just consumed with it. Once that happens, you'll be on your way to the greatest harvest of your life.

Don't Miss the Boat

I must warn you. When you set your heart to seek God and ask Him for a giving assignment, you're likely to hear a figure that shocks you as much as that $50,000 figure shocked me. If you do, don't try to reason out in your head how God can supply you with that kind of money.

Don't try to scale down His instructions and adjust them to your experience by thinking, *Well, God couldn't possibly be asking me for $50,000. That's more than I make in a year. If I gave away $50,000, I wouldn't have anything left to buy groceries!*

GOD NEVER ASKS YOU FOR MORE THAN HE CAN GIVE YOU. And if you're obedient, He'll never leave you poorer than before you gave. He'll always leave you richer.

Luke 5 gives us a picture of a man who failed to understand that principle and missed out on the most magnificent fishing trip in history. Let's take a look at it because there's something very important we can learn there.

> And it came to pass, that, as the people pressed upon him [Jesus] to hear the word of God, he stood by the lake of Gennesaret, And saw two ships standing by the lake: but the fishermen were gone out of them, and were washing their nets. And he entered into one of the ships, which was Simon's, and prayed him that he would thrust out a little from the land. And he sat down, and taught the people out of the ship. Now when he had left speaking, he said unto Simon, Launch out into the deep, and let down your nets for a draught. And Simon answering said unto him, Master, we have toiled all the night, and have taken nothing: nevertheless at thy word I will let down the net (verses 1-5).

Before you read any further, I want you to get a mental picture of what was going on here. Jesus was standing by the lake preaching, and a great crowd was pressing in to hear Him.

Simon Peter and the other fishermen, however, were not. They were within earshot, but they weren't paying much attention. They were just washing their nets.

Now washing nets is a hard job. No doubt, the only thing that was going through Peter's mind as he did it was how much he wanted to finish so he could go home, eat breakfast and get some sleep.

As you can imagine, he was probably less than thrilled when Jesus delayed him by asking to use his boat as a platform from which to preach. That in itself was bother enough. But Jesus didn't stop there. He went a step further and asked Peter to take Him fishing!

This preacher had the audacity to ask Peter, who had spent the whole night on the lake, to "Launch out into the deep, and let down your nets for a catch."

Notice Jesus said, "Let down your nets (plural) for a catch. " He didn't say, "Maybe we'll catch fish." He said, "Let's go out and get them."

How did Peter respond? He began by addressing Jesus as *Master*. Peter, at that time, had not made Jesus Lord of his life. He was using the word Master as a title like Reverend. Even at that, it wasn't much of a compliment because neither he nor the rest of those fishermen were very impressed with church. That's why they weren't paying much attention to Jesus while I Ie was preaching.

So, what Peter was actually saying was, "Reverend, we've fished all night. We didn't catch anything and neither will you. Nevertheless at thy word I will let down the net."

Look at that last word again. It's *net*. Singular.

Jesus said, Let down your *nets*. Peter said, I'll let down the *net*. Why? Because Peter, being a fisherman who had fished on that lake most of his life, *thought* he knew what would happen.

He *thought* they would not catch any fish.

He was just humoring Jesus when he said, "At thy word I will let down the net." He didn't think Jesus' word was full of power. He didn't have any idea what His word was capable of doing. In Peter's mind, Jesus was just a carpenter who had quit His business and started preaching. He certainly didn't think Jesus knew anything about fishing.

He figured, *If this preacher wants to fish, I'll let him fish. But I've been out all night and I'm tired. I am not washing all those nets again. I'll just take this one old rotten net. It's so worthless, I won't have to re-wash it when I get back to shore.*

How do we know the net was rotten? It broke, and fishing nets were not made to break when they were full. You can see that as you read the rest of the story.

> And when they had this done [launched into the deep and let down the net], they inclosed a great multitude of fishes: and their net brake. And they beckoned unto their partners, which were in the other ship, that they should come and help them. And they came, and filled both the ships, so that they began to sink (verses 6-7).

Notice the partners' nets didn't break when they were filled. That's because they had all the good nets!

Can you imagine how frustrated Peter must have been? He was standing there with every fish in the lake around his boat. They were so thick he could walk to shore on them. But he couldn't catch any because all he had was that one rotten net.

His partners were having the time of their lives, catching fish one load right after another. They filled up their boat, then they filled up Jesus and Peter's boat. "When Simon Peter saw it, he fell down at Jesus' knees, saying, Depart from me; for I am a sinful man, O Lord. For he was astonished, and all that were with him, at the draught of the fishes which they had taken" (verses 8-9).

Peter was so overwhelmed by his disobedience and lack of faith, he just fell at Jesus' knees. Why His knees and not His feet? His feet were covered up with fish!

I imagine Jesus was filled with joy and laughter as He watched Peter—fish slapping him in the face—finally receive the revelation that Jesus is not just *Reverend*—He is *Lord*.

Why not learn from Peter's experience so you don't have to end up face down in the boat of life, missing out on the blessings of God? Realize that Jesus knows what He is doing. When He leads you to give a specific amount, don't argue with Him and let your mind talk you out of it. Don't try to adjust the amount down to where it won't cost you anything.

He isn't instructing you to give that amount in order to make things hard on you. He's instructing you to do it because He is about to call all the fish in the lake to your boat. He is setting you up to be blessed beyond your wildest dreams.

So when He says *nets*, obey. When He says *Give so much*, do it His way.

Sure, you'll make mistakes sometimes. But always make your mistakes going toward God, not holding back from Him. Make your mistakes by giving too much, not too little.

Say to yourself, *Bless God, if Jesus wants my nets, I'll wash them 15 times a day if that's what it takes. I'll give Him every net I have.*

If you'll have that attitude, you'll be able to feed every poor family in the county with the boatload of blessings you bring to shore.

THE SEASONS OF PROSPERITY

10

Chapter 10

The Seasons of Prosperity

By now I pray your spiritual engines are roaring. Faith is rising in your heart and you're ready to not only read about, but you are ready to act on the Word of God concerning your finances. You're ready to prosper!

So let's take one more very practical look at this process of seed-planting and harvest. Let's examine it season by season, so you'll be sure to know exactly what to do every step of the way.

Whether you're dealing with natural things or spiritual things, seasons are important. If you plant a vegetable garden during July in West Texas where I was raised, for example, you won't accomplish much. You can plant great seed in the ground, but all you'll do is get very hot and sweaty and destroy a lot of good seed.

But you can take that same seed, plant it in soil that's been properly prepared and in the proper season, and it will yield a harvest. That's why Ecclesiastes 3:1-2 says, "To every thing there is a season, and a time to every purpose under the heaven: A time to be born, and a time to die; a time to plant, and a time to pluck up that which is planted."

Prepare the Soil

When it comes to prosperity, the first season is a time of preparation. It's a season when you take the Word of God and use it to till the soil of your heart.

Many times, people don't want to go to the trouble to do that. When they hear the message about seed-plant and harvest, they're so eager to reap a fast financial harvest that they just start throwing money in every direction. Because of skipping the preparation phase and then failing to do what's necessary to cultivate their faith, the end result is disappointment.

Don't make that mistake. Be willing to take the time and effort to search through the Bible for yourself and read what it has to say about prosperity. As you read, take note of the scriptures that especially speak to you and write them down. Put them on 3-by-5 cards, for instance, and carry them with you throughout the day. Read them and meditate on them as often as possible. Pray them aloud when you wake up in the morning. Then pray them aloud again before you go to bed at night.

Train yourself to think according to those scriptures every day. Remember, you've spent years thinking the world's way, so it will take some diligence to retrain your mind. You won't be able to get the job done by saying, "Glory to God, I believe God is going to prosper me," and then not giving it another thought for six months. You'll have to stay with it.

This season of preparation is also the time to become very specific about what you need. Don't settle for knowing generally that you need "more money." Target your faith. Figure out how much income it would take not only to meet your family's expenses, but also to increase your standard of living to where it should be to tithe and to give as God directs you. Specify that amount and write it down. Don't get stupid, but at the same time, don't be cheap. You won't impress God either way.

That's important because if you fluctuate without being specific, one day saying, "Oh, I set that too high. That's too much for little ole me." Then a few days later and a tape or so later, you get all excited and go for 20 miles the other side of the moon, your faith won't know what to produce. That specific amount has become your hope, and faith is the substance of things hoped for. For as James 1:6-8 says, "...He that wavereth is like a wave of the sea driven with the wind and tossed. For let not that man think that he shall receive any thing of the Lord. A double minded man is unstable in all his ways."

"Well, Brother Copeland, I don't think I need to believe God for anything specific financially. After all, He knows what I need better than I do. I just think I'll leave it up to Him."

Do you know what will happen if you do that? Very little, that's what!

God has already done everything He is going to do about your prosperity. He sent Jesus who went to the cross and became poor, that you "through his poverty might be rich" (2 Corinthians 8:9). He gave you His Word that He will meet your needs. He has made heaven's supply available, but it's up to you to tap in to that supply by faith, and faith is specific.

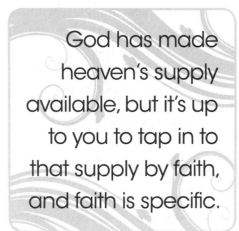

God has made heaven's supply available, but it's up to you to tap in to that supply by faith, and faith is specific.

Mark 11:24 reveals just how specific it is. There Jesus told His disciples, "...What things soever ye desire, when ye pray, believe that ye receive them, and ye shall have them." Again in Philippians 4:6, the Lord instructs us: "Do not fret or have any anxiety about anything, but in every circumstance and in every-thing by prayer and petition [definite requests] with thanksgiving continue to make your wants known to God" (Philippians 4:6, *The Amplified Bible*).

If you don't believe specifically, you will not receive specific results. For as Jesus said, "According to your faith be it unto you" (Matthew 9:29).

Actually, that's spiritual law. You can see it in operation throughout the earthly ministry of Jesus. He had the Spirit of God without measure. That means He could do anything on this Earth that the Father God Himself could do. Yet Jesus didn't just walk around meeting the needs of everyone He met.

In a crowd of thousands, He might stop and respond to a single individual. We know He cared about every individual, and we know that He "is no respecter of persons" (Acts 10:34). What was it then that caused Him to respond to one person differently than another?

Faith. Not the general kind of faith that acknowledges God's power, but the kind of faith that is released when a person believes God can and will meet a particular need.

It's that kind of faith that directed Jesus' ministry. Mark 5, for instance, tells of a time when Jesus was teaching the crowds by the seashore and a man named Jairus pushed his way through to Him. Falling at Jesus' feet, he said, "My little daughter lieth at the point of death: I pray thee, come and lay thy hands on her, that she may be healed; and she shall live" (verse 23).

Notice Jairus didn't say, "Jesus, my little girl is sick, but I don't want to put any demands on You. After all, You're the Son of God. You know better than I what should happen. So just do whatever You think is best."

No, Jairus was very specific in what he wanted from Jesus. He said, "Come lay Your hands on her and she will be healed and live." In response to those words of faith, Jesus left the crowd and went with Jairus. One man's faith changed the direction of His ministry.

On the way to Jairus' house, so many people pressed around Jesus that He could hardly move. But He kept walking until suddenly, something stopped Him. What was it? *The touch of faith!*

A woman who had been suffering from a flow of blood for 12 years had pushed her way through the crowd saying, "If I may touch but his clothes, I shall be whole" (verse 28).

Once again, notice this dear lady didn't lie at home in her sickbed saying, "Well, God knows I'm sick. If it's His will to heal me, He's perfectly able to send Jesus to my house today. So I'll just wait here and see what happens."

On the contrary, this woman fought her way through a crushing mob of people, believing in her heart and saying with her mouth exactly what she expected to receive from Jesus.

Can we be sure that was the key to her healing? Yes, because Jesus, Himself turned to her and said, "Daughter, thy faith hath made thee whole..." (verse 34).

In Mark 10, we see blind Bartimaeus so confident that he would receive the specific thing he was believing for that he threw off his coat—the garment that identified him as a blind man and gave him license to beg for a living—*before* he was healed! "And Jesus said unto him, Go thy way; thy faith hath made thee whole..." (verse 52).

In Matthew 9:28-29, Jesus asked two men, "Believe ye that I am able to do this? They said unto him, Yea, Lord. Then touched he their eyes, saying, According to your faith be it unto you."

Why didn't Jesus say, "According to *My* faith be it done unto you"? Didn't Jesus have any faith? Certainly He did! "Without faith it is impossible to please him [God]..." (Hebrews 11:6)—and the Bible says Jesus pleased God perfectly.

There's no question that Jesus had and used His faith. His faith connection to God was never broken. He was always full of the Holy Ghost and power. He was always anointed. But for that power and anointing to be delivered to someone, it had to be touched by the faith of someone who was believing for a specific result. Our faith is our connection to His anointing.

A Heavenly Grant

Being specific in your faith will not only enable you to receive from God, it will also help you defeat the devil more effectively when he tries to discourage you. Every time the devil tells you, *You'll never have enough money to make ends meet*, you can answer him with facts and figures. You can say, "Yes I will, devil. God is providing me with $5,000 a month and that's enough to pay my bills, bless my family and give into the kingdom of God!"

I learned the value of that early in my ministry. I recall one time in particular when my dad, who was directing our office, figured up the amount we needed each month to keep the ministry going. It doesn't sound like much now for an entire ministry to operate on, but back then $5,000 a month took my breath away. I didn't know there was that much money in the whole world!

So I opened my Bible and read in John 16:23 where Jesus said, "...I assure you, most solemnly I tell you, that My Father will grant you whatever you ask in My name..." *(The Amplified Bible)*. Then I turned to Mark 11:24 and read, "...Whatever you ask for in prayer, believe—trust and be confident—that it is granted to you, and you will [get it]" *(The Amplified Bible)*.

Well, that settles it, I thought. *According to the Word, I can obtain a heavenly grant! I simply need to ask for what I need in Jesus' Name, then believe I receive it and it will be mine.* So I wrote down the amount I needed, thanked God for it and considered it done.

A few days later, my dad called me on the phone. He was at the office and he had paid bills until we ran out of money. The problem was, there were still bills unpaid. "What do you want me to do?" he asked.

"Just go home and don't worry about it," I answered. "I have already believed for and received by faith a heavenly grant from God that will cover those bills." Of course, I was speaking out of my spirit because my mind was giving me all kinds of problems. It was racing around wondering how God could get this money to us in time. But I ignored that and simply confessed what I believed in my heart.

After my dad hung up the phone and began preparing to close the office for the day, a woman walked through the front door of the office waving a check. "Take this right now!" she said. "God told me to give you this money several days ago and I didn't do it. Just a few minutes ago I was sitting in my car at a traffic light and the Lord spoke to me so strongly it shook me. He told me to get this check to you immediately!"

As you can imagine, that thrilled me. But I didn't get to sit back and enjoy that thrill very long because the ministry grew quickly, and very soon I had to go back and apply for a bigger grant from God.

That's the way it always is in faith. You can never just rest on your laurels. You can never lean back and think, *Well, we're in "Fat City" now. We have arrived! We don't have to use our faith anymore.* No, if you go with God, you'll always be growing. Eventually you'll learn to believe God for increase, not because your back is against the wall financially, but because you want to give more and do more for the kingdom of God. That's when the going really gets good!

Put Your Seed in the Ground

Once you've prepared the soil of your heart by meditating the Word and you know specifically what you need from God, you're ready to move into the next season in this process of seed-plant and harvest. You're ready to take your request to God and pray the prayer of faith.

I suggest you write it down like a formal petition. Include exactly what you're believing God for and the scriptures upon

> Seek the Lord
> for His wisdom
> and guidance
> about where to
> sow the seed.

which you are basing your faith. If you're married, you and your spouse can get on your knees in prayer together and bring that request before God.

For years, that's how Gloria and I have dealt with every significant need in our ministry. We would go directly to the Word of God and read aloud the scriptures that covered our need. Then we would write our prayer of agreement down in a notebook and pray it out loud together before God, setting ourselves in agreement according to Matthew 18:19 which says, "...If two of you shall agree on earth as touching any thing that they shall ask, it shall be done for them of my Father which is in heaven."

Once you've prayed the prayer of faith and believed you've received, you have planted the seed of your faith toward your prosperity. Next comes the action of planting the material representation of that seed in the form of a gift.

At this point bless your seed. Whatever you have determined to give, lay your hands on it. Write the check or place the cash on the altar of your faith before God. If there is no money, don't be discouraged. Search for something to give. God is the provider of seed as well as the harvest (2 Corinthians 9:10).

Begin to seek the Lord for His wisdom and guidance about where to sow the seed. His direction is of great importance because you have just given your seed to Him. In the spirit, you have already planted it. It's His so it must be placed where He wants it. Listen. Listen. Listen. Obedience is greater than sacrifice. Now release it! Begin watering it with your praise and worship. Now it's time to begin speaking to your harvest.

Command it to come to you in Jesus' Name.

I realize that sounds strange to most people but Jesus taught this. He spoke to the fig tree in Mark 11:14. He said, "No man eat fruit of thee hereafter for ever...." As a result, that tree withered up from the roots. Then when His disciples questioned Him about it, He explained to them that speaking to things in faith was a spiritual principle that would work for anyone who would use it.

> For verily I say unto you, That whosoever shall say unto this mountain, Be thou removed, and be thou cast into the sea; and shall not doubt in his heart, but shall believe that those things which he saith shall come to pass; he shall have whatsoever he saith (Mark 11:23).

Once you've spoken to the money, speak to the devil. Bind him according to Matthew 18:18 and command him in Jesus' Name to keep his hands off your harvest. Many people fail to do that and the devil, being the thief that he is, slips in and steals what God sends them. Then they walk around crying about how God never blesses them financially.

God *has* blessed them. He *sent* their supply. The devil just stole it from them. Their failure to follow Jesus' instruction in the Word is the problem—not God!

Think of it this way. What if you were to receive a monthly dividend check from a company that managed your investments for you, but every month when that check came, the guy next door beat you to your mailbox and stole it. Would it do you any good to call the investment company and complain that you never receive your check?

No, it wouldn't. To change the situation, you'd have to deal with that thief next door. You'd have to bring in the authorities and stop him from taking your money.

The same thing is true in the spiritual realm. In obedience to Jesus' commands, you must take authority over the devil and all of his principalities and powers. You have to slap him down with the Word of God. Every time you give a gift, say, "Devil, I bind you in the Name of Jesus. *I'm a tither* and the Word says you are rebuked for my sake. You can't touch my harvest!"

But don't stop there. Matthew 18:18 not only says, "Whatsoever ye shall bind on earth shall be bound in heaven," it also says, "whatsoever ye shall loose on earth shall be loosed in heaven." So once you've bound the devil, loose the angels of God to go to work bringing in your harvest. You have a scriptural right to do that because Hebrews 1:14 tells us that angels are "all ministering spirits, sent forth to minister for them who shall be heirs of salvation."

How do you loose your angels? Psalm 103:20 says they hearken to the voice of God's Word, so speak the Word to them. They'll immediately go to work on your behalf. (The Name of Jesus is in authority over all the world of the spirit, not just the devil's part—Philippians 2:10).

If you're in real estate, your angels might go out and impress people to do business with you. Some fellow you haven't heard from in years might call you up and say, "I've been wanting to sell some land and your name kept coming to my mind. Would you be interested in listing it for me?"

You're more familiar with how angels work than you realize because in the past they've worked with you! Maybe you were just driving down the road one day when suddenly, out of the blue, this thought came to you, *Send Kenneth Copeland Ministries some money,* or *Your pastor needs a new suit.* Maybe you decided, *Yes, I'll do that,* but then you got busy with other things and forgot about it. So a couple of days later, you were brushing your teeth when the thought came again, *Send Kenneth Copeland*

Ministries some money. Your pastor needs a new suit.

What was that? That was an angel at work revealing good seed and good ground, revealing God's desires and responding to your pastor's and my faith! Be obedient to their call because your angels are out there to prosper your way.

Actually, the devil works the same way. As an angel who was once in God's employ, He knew God's system. After he fell, he perverted that system and used it to tempt and pressure people by firing thoughts at people with the force of a machine gun.

The angels of God, however, never put you under pressure. They'll tell you something, then they'll leave you alone. If you aren't paying attention, they'll come back later and tell you again. But if you don't want to hear what they have to say, they'll back off completely and go deal with someone else instead. The person who does listen will reap the harvest that you passed up.

Keep Accurate Records

One more thing I suggest you do during the season of the planting of your seed is keep a written record not only of what you give, but of the harvest you are expecting. Don't take the lazy attitude some people do and say, "Well, God knows what I give and He'll be faithful."

Certainly, God will be faithful. You aren't keeping records for His benefit, you are keeping them for yours! You should know how much you've put in God's bank. It's poor stewardship not to know what your resources are. It's also poor stewardship not to have named your seed when you planted it. As I said earlier, know what you are expecting.

If you give $100 and you're believing for the hundredfold return, write down $10,000. You have $10,000 in your heavenly account! It's there to call upon when you have need. It's there to stand on in faith when lack tries to force its way into your thoughts. It is yours. Act like it. Talk like it. Rest in it in the peace of God.

Don't try to *make it* come into your hands. *Let it* come into your hands. When you try to make things happen you get in God's way. When you rejoice in the Lord and let things happen, all of heaven is working in your behalf.

> The more you speak the Word, the more you'll hear it. The more you hear it, the more faith will rise up in your heart.

Soak the Soil

After you've completed the season of seed-planting, you'll be ready to move into the season of growth. What must you do during that season? First and foremost, you must keep the soil wet by soaking it with the Word and praise.

Put living water on your seed by speaking God's Word all day long. That may sound extreme, but it's scriptural because Psalm 35:27 tells us to "...say continually, Let the Lord be magnified, which hath pleasure in the prosperity of his servant."

Walk around all day saying, "Praise God, the harvest is mine. I have it. The angels of God are out there gathering it up, praise God. I have planted my seed in the kingdom of God and the harvest is mine whether the devil likes it or not!"

When you first begin to make such confessions, they may feel somewhat empty. That's because your heart hasn't taken hold of them completely by faith yet, and they're still partly coming out of your mind. But don't let that discourage you. Keep on confessing the Word anyway because faith comes by hearing and hearing by the Word of God (see Romans 10:17).

The more you speak the Word, the more you'll hear it. The more you hear it, the more faith will rise up in your heart and expel the worldly ideas about prosperity you've stored in there over the years.

That's the primary reason you need to make those confessions continually. It's not because you're trying to make God do something. He is faithful to His Word and you don't have to push Him into keeping it by making a thousand confessions. Remember that and when you confess the Word, just rest in God. Relax in knowing that Word is at work watering your seed and changing your heart.

Of course, the devil will try to stop you by saying, *You might as well quit this confessing business. It makes you look like a fool and it's not doing any good anyway. After all, nothing is happening.*

But don't fall for his tricks. He just wants you to quit because he knows what will happen if the Word of God keeps coming out of your mouth. He's defeated and losing ground!

So don't quit. Just keep on speaking the Word, and eventually those confessions will come out of the abundance of your heart without your mind having anything to do with it. When that happens, brace yourself. All the demons of hell will start running from you and everything good will start coming to you.

You'll jump and shout and rejoice because you'll know with all your heart that your harvest is coming and there's nothing that can stop it. It is signed, sealed and delivered. When that happens, confession becomes easy. It just flows out of your mouth as a praise to God.

If you haven't known the power of confessing the Word until now, you may have a lot of seed out there that's never had any water on it. You may have been giving for years, just plunking your offering in the bucket when it goes past. You've been dry-land farming when you could have been irrigating with the Word of God.

Don't give up on that seed! It's still in the ground. Go back and reclaim it by putting the water of the Word on it. You'll be amazed at what will grow!

There's one final word you need to remember when it comes to keeping your soil watered. It comes from 1 Kings 8:35-36. There, King Solomon, as he prayed over the newly built temple, revealed an important truth that applies to us today as surely as it did to the Israelites back then.

> When heaven is shut up, and there is no rain, because they [God's people] have sinned against thee; if they pray...and confess thy name, and turn from their sin, when [they are afflicted]: Then hear thou in heaven, and forgive the sin of thy servants, and of thy people Israel, that thou teach them the good way wherein they should walk, and give rain upon thy land, which thou hast given to thy people for an inheritance.

Sin stops the rain of God's spirit. It doesn't matter how much you give or how many times you confess the Word, if you're living in disobedience to God, you will not prosper.

So stay sensitive to God's Spirit. Fellowship with Him in the Word and in prayer, and ask Him to reveal any areas of your life that are out of line. When He does, be quick to repent, receive forgiveness through the blood of Jesus, and make the necessary changes. Keep the rain of God's anointing flowing freely in *every* area of your life.

Having Done All...Stand

"But Brother Copeland, what should I do when I've prepared

my soil, planted my seed, kept it watered with the Word and my harvest still hasn't come?"

You follow the instructions in Ephesians 6:13-14, "...Having done all, to stand. Stand therefore...." You keep walking by faith every day. You keep believing God is faithful to His Word. You keep praising Him for your harvest. Rejoice in the Lord—always. Rejoicing in the Lord and not in the way things look or feel is rejoicing by faith. In the Lord things are always *good*.

In other words, you stand—and stand—and stand.

How long?

As long as it takes.

I'll warn you, during that standing time every kind of discouragement will come your way. The devil will throw one circumstance after another at you to prove to you God's Word won't work for you. He'll pressure you to drop your faith and hunt for natural solutions.

Believe me, I know that from experience. There have been times when I've stepped out on the platform to preach and the devil was right there telling me, *Boy, you better do something fast. You're $1,000 behind your budget and those people out there aren't listening to God. You'd better make an appeal to them. You'd better tell them you need their help or you're going under.*

When he says things like that to you, just slap him in the head with the Word of God and keep right on standing and rejoicing.

Genesis 15:11 tells of the time when Abraham had laid his covenant sacrifices before God, and the birds of prey tried to eat those sacrifices. But he drove them away. He absolutely refused to let those predators steal his covenant offering.

You'll have to be the same way. You'll have to fight the buzzards off your harvest. You'll have to drive off every thought of doubt and unbelief with words of faith.

"Well, that sounds difficult to me!"

Certainly it is. If it were easy, everybody would be doing it.

It takes commitment, dedication and total surrender to do this. You must be so determined to become what God wants you to be that like the Apostle Paul, you consider yourself a "prisoner of Jesus Christ" (Philemon 1).

If you and I are to prosper in God enough to bring in the resources we need to finish the job that's facing us, we must give ourselves to Him completely. We won't be able to do it by just praying really hard when things are bad and forgetting it when they're good. We've come as far as we can with that kind of lackadaisical attitude toward the things of God.

God needs people in this day and hour who will make this seed-plant and harvest process a lifestyle, people who don't just try it for a while and then quit but who will live it every day for the rest of their lives no matter what it takes. He needs people He can trust with material things. He needs people who will give more than they keep for themselves, people who will, regardless of the cost, see to it that the gospel is preached around the world.

He is searching to and fro throughout the whole Earth in order to show Himself strong in behalf of people like that (2 Chronicles 16:9). He is finding them too. And one day very soon, He will stagger the world with the riches and resources He empowers into their hands.

> **If you and I are to prosper in God enough to bring in the resources we need to finish the job facing us, we must give ourselves to Him completely.**

He will give to them the wealth of the wicked that has been laid up for the just. He will cause the glory of the latter house to be so much greater than that of the former house that the prosperity of the Church of the Lord Jesus Christ will outshine anything this Earth has ever seen.

It will happen. The Bible says so. There's no question about it. In fact it has already begun.

I've made up my mind and my heart that when it does, Gloria and I will be right in the middle of it. How about you?

Rejoice! And again I say rejoice! The future is now!

11

THE BLESSING DISTRIBUTORS

Chapter 11

THE BLESSING *Distributors*

As you begin to meditate on and apply the Bible principles and promises we've looked at, a shift in perspective will begin to take place in your thinking. You'll see God desires more than for you to just tap in to heaven's resources. His dream is for you to live out of a continual flow of heaven's supply—to live in and give to others out of an entirely different system. He not only wants you to experience the blessings of heaven—He wants you to live in and be a distributor of His BLESSING system throughout the whole earth.

You remember that, as we looked at God's purpose for prosperity, we saw He desires to bless His people so they can be a blessing. We discovered He gives us power to get wealth, so He may establish His covenant (Deuteronomy 8:18) and so we "may have to give to him that needeth" (Ephesians 4:28).

God has freed us from the world's cycle of greed and lack and from worrying about where the next meal will come from and what clothes we will wear (Matthew 6). And He has opened our eyes to His system in which we have "all sufficiency in all things"—so we may have enough to "abound to every good work" (2 Corinthians 9:8).

Every system of man not built on God's love and dream for him is built on a foundation of sand and will fall. It is a house built in vain. Only in God's system will man ever find the firm footing and lasting security of a system not funded by lack, debt, bondage and control through fear—a system that draws directly from heaven's unlimited provision and God's unconditional love...the Eden system.

When the world system buckles and finds itself increasingly

incapable of propping itself back up, it should not be a distraction to the believer whose house is built on the rock of THE BLESSING God first spoke over Adam and restored to us, when Jesus took the curse of sin into His own body on the cross.

Let's look at those first words Adam ever heard—words that equipped, empowered and defined his assignment on the earth: "And God blessed them, and God said unto them, Be fruitful, and multiply, and replenish the earth, and subdue it: and have dominion over the fish of the sea, and over the fowl of the air, and over every living thing that moveth upon the earth" (Genesis 1:28).

Do you see any sickness in those words? Any poverty? Any hopelessness? No. You see everything needed to live in the fullness of what prosperity really is.

By THE BLESSING He breathed into man at Creation, God empowered and assigned man to take every benefit of the Garden of Eden—which had no sickness, no lack, no darkness or confusion—to the whole earth.

Even after man's fall into sin, that BLESSING assignment never changed. In Genesis 9:1, the Bible says: "And God blessed Noah and his sons, and said unto them, Be fruitful, and multiply, and replenish the earth."

And today, the empowering to complete that assignment is what Jesus bore for us on the cross: "Christ hath redeemed us from the curse of the law, being made a curse for us: for it is written, Cursed is every one that hangeth on a tree: that the blessing of Abraham might come on the Gentiles through Jesus Christ; that we might receive the promise of the Spirit through faith" (Galatians 3:13-14).

God's Dream Has Not Changed

You see, despite the challenges and changes the world system goes through, one thing will never change: God is the same yesterday, today and forever. And according to Isaiah 51:2-3, His dream for man has never changed. He has a way for us to get through the mess we have created: "Look unto Abraham your father, and unto Sarah that bare you: for I called him alone, and blessed him, and increased him. For the Lord shall comfort Zion: he will comfort all her waste places; and he will make her wilderness like Eden, and her desert like the garden of the Lord; joy and gladness shall be found therein, thanksgiving, and the voice of melody."

God's dream for man is just as true today as it was when the prophet first delivered those words. I don't care who we are, where we've come from or what we've done, the only reason it has not turned out as God desires is not because of Him, but because of our disobedience and the choosing of our own way.

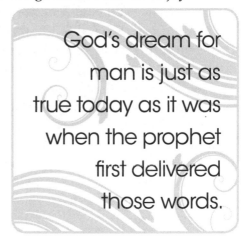

God's dream for man is just as true today as it was when the prophet first delivered those words.

Instead of giving up on fallen man, God gives us the way through what we've created. To paraphrase those same verses: "Forsake your way of thinking and follow after righteousness. Seek the Lord. Look to Abraham. I chose him. I blessed him. And I will make his desert—Abraham's descendants and My people—like Eden."

THE BLESSING of Abraham is the Eden Blessing. It is the Eden promise and assignment (Genesis 1:28).

It is the Eden way—the Eden system of bringing the Garden to the whole earth. Just as God brought what was seen into existence by His Word, we too should be saying what He has said to restore His plan of abundance and peace first to our own lives, and then to our world:

> For verily I say unto you, That whosoever shall say unto this mountain, Be thou removed, and be thou cast into the sea; and shall not doubt in his heart, but shall believe that those things which he saith shall come to pass; he shall have whatsoever he saith. Therefore I say unto you, What things soever ye desire, when ye pray, believe that ye receive them, and ye shall have them (Mark 11:23-24).

That is the Eden system—God's way for His people to bless the whole earth by unleashing the provision of heaven. God's promise to make our deserts and waste places like Eden belongs to every born-again man and woman who will take it by faith.

Our task is not to get back to Eden, but to get the Eden Blessing back in us—to develop and expand it throughout the whole earth.

Babylon's System Has Failed

One reason Christians have had such a hard time understanding the true purpose and meaning of prosperity is they have viewed it through what the world has taught us. They have assumed that the world's system is the only one we have to work with. The world's system was brought about by Adam's fall, ultimately manifesting as an alternate system of doing things without God, first seen in the attempt to build the tower of Babel in Genesis 11:1-4:

> And the whole earth was of one language, and of one

speech. And it came to pass, as they journeyed from the east, that they found a plain in the land of Shinar; and they dwelt there. And they said one to another, Go to, let us make brick, and burn them thoroughly. And they had brick for stone, and slime had they for mortar. And they said, Go to, let us build us a city and a tower, whose top may reach unto heaven; and let us make us a name, lest we be scattered abroad upon the face of the whole earth.

The Bible says the people were all of one language, and said, "Let us build us a city and a tower, whose top may reach unto heaven; and let us make us a name." At that time man, even fallen man, only knew one system: Imagine it, believe it, speak it, have it.

They were using the Eden system for something other than the Eden assignment. And it was working. God said so in verse 6 of that chapter: "Behold, the people is one, and they have all one language; and this they begin to do: and now nothing will be restrained from them, which they have imagined to do."

Despite what was happening, God never reversed His commitment to man or changed His way for man to bless the earth with heaven's resources. Instead, He spoke one word—*babel*, or confusion—putting a cap on what they could imagine. He put a limit on the ability of fallen man—whose thoughts were already dominated by death, fear and sin—to think the same thing long enough to finish a task not anchored in His Word. Man could no longer control his imagination without the power of God. He forever confounded the languages of men so they could no longer understand each other's speech.

Out of that confusion has come the Babylonian system—the world's way of doing things.

Remember, the people building that tower were descendants

of two of Noah's sons—Ham and Japheth. Ham and Japheth, along with their older brother, Shem—were present with their father after the Flood when the first words man heard were the same BLESSING spoken to Adam: "And God blessed Noah and his sons, and said unto them, Be fruitful, and multiply, and replenish the earth" (Genesis 9:1).

Two Systems Instead of One

Though Ham and Japheth did not stay with THE BLESSING, Shem did. He lived 502 years after the Flood and became patriarch of Israel and founder of Salem (which later became Jerusalem). According to Jewish history, Melchizedek, the high priest of God who spoke God's promise over Abraham, was Shem. Melchizedek was king of Salem and high priest—speaker for the Most High God before his generations. So it was Shem, the son of Noah whom God had blessed, who came to Abraham with the elements of covenant and blessed him, saying: "Blessed be Abram of the most high God, possessor of heaven and earth: And blessed be the most high God, which hath delivered thine enemies into thy hand" (Genesis 14:19-20).

Shem was speaking to his descendant, Abraham, THE BLESSING spoken to him and his father and brothers—the Eden Blessing. Shem was not declaring God the possessor of heaven and earth, but Abraham. The descendants of Ham and Japheth (the gentiles) were spreading confusion worldwide and their life system was not based on a covenant with God. But by the elements of covenant—the bread and the wine—Shem anchored Abraham's soul to the reality of the Eden Blessing in a way Abraham could never forget: "Abraham believed God, and it was counted unto him for righteousness" (Romans 4:3).

And because he received by faith, he opened the door for God's dream to be restored not just to the descendants of Shem, but to the gentiles—the descendants of Ham and Japheth. That's you and me, who through faith in Jesus would become the seed of Abraham and heirs according to the promise.

Only when we fully understand God's dream, to see all men and women restored to Him and the abundance He has prepared for them, can we appreciate what Jesus did for us on the cross:

"For the promise, that he should be the heir of the world, was not to Abraham, or to his seed, through the law, but through the righteousness of faith. Therefore it is of faith, that it might be by grace; to the end the promise might be sure to all the seed; not to that only which is of the law, but to that also which is of the faith of Abraham; who is the father of us all" (Romans 4:13, 16).

"There is neither Jew nor Greek, there is neither bond nor free, there is neither male nor female: for ye are all one in Christ Jesus. And if ye be Christ's, then are ye Abraham's seed, and heirs according to the promise" (Galatians 3:28-29).

By His blood, Jesus has made a way for every man, woman and child who believes, to live by the Eden system instead of the Babylonian system.

Commissioned to Bless

The Babylonian system came into being through Ham and Japheth. It is simply man attempting to meet his own needs—spirit, soul, body and financially—without God. It offers a spiritual, yet godless, way to meet man's spiritual needs: It's called religion, and it doesn't work. It has its own healing system, its own financial system, its own educational system, but none of them work. Out of that system comes racism, crying and death. All the sorrow of the curse on this planet is under that system, and it's still functioning today.

Though many Christians believe the world system is the only one they have to work with, there is another way—it's

> We live under Eden's system—a system that operates by faith, hope and love, not domination and control through fear.

called the Eden system.

As believers, we don't have any business being trapped in that Babylonian system—a system which motivates and controls people by fear. We live under Eden's system—a system that operates by faith, hope and love, not domination and control through fear. Eden's system—spiritually, emotionally, socially and in every other way—is based on the promises and abundance of God's covenant of love, protection and provision. It's a system of giving, as God directs and supplies from heaven's resources, not hoarding for fear of lack.

Under the Eden system, believers quit focusing on provision and start focusing on THE BLESSING assignment in their lives. We learn to exercise the faith of Abraham, who "being not weak in faith, he considered not his own body now dead, when he was about an hundred years old, neither yet the deadness of Sarah's womb: He staggered not at the promise of God through unbelief; but was strong in faith, giving glory to God; and being fully persuaded that, what he had promised, he was able also to perform" (Romans 4:19-21). Therefore, he became heir of the world, not by works, but by faith (see Romans 4:13).

Abraham believed what God said, and God counted it as righteousness. In other words, God treated him as if he had never sinned. And God will treat every believer who believes

Him and does what He says, the same way. God is in the business of forgiving and wiping out sin so that THE BLESSING can take over in our lives.

Our part is to believe what God said, then act on it—so we can take our place in the promise and assignment that we, too, have been made heirs of the world.

That is the blessing Jesus was speaking over us as He ascended into heaven. He was blessing reborn man as a new generation in this earth. He was blessing the generation of born-again believers, filled with His Spirit, who would walk this earth, not speaking out of the confusion of every man's own fear-driven thoughts, but instead, speaking the same thing God has said. He blessed us with the Eden Blessing, saying, "Go ye into every nation everywhere, and in every way the world system has held them in bondage and fear, bring them the Eden Blessing."

The Garden of Eden was never meant to be the highest expression of life in God—it was supposed to be just the starting point. "For since the beginning of the world men have not heard, nor perceived by the ear, neither hath the eye seen, O God, beside thee, what he hath prepared for him that waiteth for him" (Isaiah 64:4).

This is the prosperity God has promised to release through those who will believe Him and walk in the fullness of what He desires to give to all He so deeply loves, that He gave His own Son for them.

His dream is for you to turn every manifestation of the devil's wasteland into Eden's Garden and release joy, gladness, thanksgiving and the joy of melody throughout this planet!

God is filling the earth with His glory through a Body of believers who have learned how to walk in the fullness of His love. He is committed to releasing heaven's abundance of healing, finances, restored relationships and realized dreams in the midst of the mess man has created.

And for those of us who will join forces with Him, we haven't seen anything yet. God has not spent the past century leaving His people unprepared for this day. No, He has been preparing the Body of Christ to purge fear from their lives by obeying His command to walk in love, and has begun focusing His people on learning how to carry out the Eden command to be a worldwide blessing.

The fullness of THE BLESSING is manifesting in prosperity of fullness in spirit, soul, body, finances and relationships—in every area of life—for those who refuse to let go of God's dream for them, and choose to focus on the purpose and blessing Jesus came to restore. It is being increasingly displayed beyond what we could ask or think in those willing to be living testimonies of God's Blessing covenant and worldwide distributors of His goodness.

Truly, we are...

Blessed to Be a Blessing!

Prayer for Salvation and Baptism in the Holy Spirit

Heavenly Father, I come to You in the Name of Jesus. Your Word says, "Whosoever shall call on the name of the Lord shall be saved" (Acts 2:21). I am calling on You. I pray and ask Jesus to come into my heart and be Lord over my life according to Romans 10:9-10: "If thou shalt confess with thy mouth the Lord Jesus, and shalt believe in thine heart that God hath raised him from the dead, thou shalt be saved. For with the heart man believeth unto righteousness; and with the mouth confession is made unto salvation." I do that now. I confess that Jesus is Lord, and I believe in my heart that God raised Him from the dead.

I am now reborn! I am a Christian—a child of Almighty God! I am saved! You also said in Your Word, "If ye then, being evil, know how to give good gifts unto your children: HOW MUCH MORE shall your heavenly Father give the Holy Spirit to them that ask him?" (Luke 11:13). I'm also asking You to fill me with the Holy Spirit. Holy Spirit, rise up within me as I praise God. I fully expect to speak with other tongues as You give me the utterance (Acts 2:4). In Jesus' Name. Amen!

Begin to praise God for filling you with the Holy Spirit. Speak those words and syllables you receive—not in your own language, but the language given to you by the Holy Spirit. You have to use your own voice. God will not force you to speak. Don't be concerned with how it sounds. It is a heavenly language!

Continue with the blessing God has given you and pray in the spirit every day.

You are a born-again, Spirit-filled believer. You'll never be the same!

Find a good church that boldly preaches God's Word and obeys it. Become part of a church family who will love and care for you as you love and care for them.

We need to be connected to each other. It increases our strength in God. It's God's plan for us.

Make it a habit to watch the *Believer's Voice of Victory* television broadcast and become a doer of the Word, who is blessed in his doing (James 1:22-25).

About the Author

Kenneth Copeland is co-founder and president of Kenneth Copeland Ministries in Fort Worth, Texas, and best-selling author of books that include *How to Discipline Your Flesh and Honor—Walking in Honesty, Truth and Integrity.*

Since 1967, Kenneth has been a minister of the gospel of Christ and teacher of God's Word. He is also the artist on award-winning albums such as his Grammy-nominated *Only the Redeemed, In His Presence, He Is Jehovah, Just a Closer Walk* and his most recently released *Big Band Gospel album.* He also co-stars as the character Wichita Slim in the children's adventure videos *The Gunslinger, Covenant Rider* and the movie *The Treasure of Eagle Mountain,* and as Daniel Lyon in the Commander Kellie and the Superkids™ videos *Armor of Light* and *Judgment: The Trial of Commander Kellie.* Kenneth also co-stars as a Hispanic godfather in the 2009 movie *The Rally.*

With the help of offices and staff in the United States, Canada, England, Australia, South Africa, Ukraine and Singapore, Kenneth is fulfilling his vision to boldly preach the uncompromised Word of God from the top of this world, to the bottom, and all the way around. His ministry reaches millions of people worldwide through daily and Sunday TV broadcasts, magazines, teaching audios and videos, conventions and campaigns, and the World Wide Web.

Learn more about Kenneth Copeland Ministries
by visiting our website at **kcm.org**